out of the dark
into the light

LOVE and LIGHT

julie watts

 pencil

ISBN 978-93-5667-098-3

Published in India 2022 by Pencil

Contributors:
Co-Author: MY SPIRIT GUIDES
Co-Author: MY SPIRIT GUIDES
Co-Author: MY SPIRIT GUIDES

A brand of
One Point Six Technologies Pvt. Ltd.
123, Building J2, Shram Seva Premises,
Wadala Truck Terminal, Wadala (E)
Mumbai 400037, Maharashtra, INDIA
E connect@thepencilapp.com
W www.thepencilapp.com

DISCLAIMER: *The opinions expressed in this book are those of the authors and do not purport to reflect the views of the Publisher.*

Author biography

I AM THE LIGHT.

If I can give you any advice, it would be to always shine as bright as you can. There is no one out there that is going to do it for you, you can do anything you want to as long as you believe you can.

Make sure to always shine that bright light you have inside of you, because it is so BRIGHT, it shines like no other. Make sure you remember to give yourself the time you need to heal from all the dark this world may have inflicted upon you, never let anyone dim your light. Breathe in all the goodness this world has to offer, it provides what you need when you need it.

Shine so bright that the rest of the world can see you for thousands of miles and don't be scared, as this is what you were meant to be, the light that brings all other light beings to where they are meant to be too.

I LOVE who I am, I am the light, I shine so bright that the world can see me everywhere. Say these affirmations before going to bed and first thing in the morning, this will help you to begin to believe that you are the light, and nothing will dim your light as long as you believe.

My light is your light, your light is my light, we are one we belong together as a whole, this world needs us to be the LIGHT.

LET THERE BE LOVE, LET THERE BE LIGHT, LET THE WHOLE WORLD SHINE SO BRIGHT SO IT CAN HEAL TOO.

CONTENTS

Epigraph

OUT OF THE DARK INTO THE LIGHT

A journey though the life of a child, young lady into a self-discovered middle aged women.

ALWAYS LOVE

NEVER FORGET WHO YOU ARE

BE THE LIGHT THAT IS WITHIN YOU

DREAM BIG

BECOME THE BEST VERTION OF YOURSELF

MAKE EVERY MOMENT COUNT

NEVER FORGET TO LIVE LIFE TO THE FULL

SOUL SEARCH

DANCE AND SING LIKE YOUR LIFE DEPENDED ON IT

LOVE

BE YOURSELF

JULIE WATTS

Preface

LETER TO THE ONES I LOVE.

To the ones I LOVE

From my heart to yours, I have been on a journey of self-discovery, I have found that not only do life have everything you could ever want and need, I have also discovered that I can do anything I set my mind to.

Lee-Andrew, If I could tell you anything, it would be to go with that gut feeling you get when you feel that there is more to life than what you are doing at this present moment in time. You have the gift inside of you that we all have, I know you feel it because you have told me so.

You need to go within and find that answer that you so long for in your heart, the one that has been niggling at you for some time now. Take it from me, it wont stop until you listen to it is trying to tell you, you can do it you just need to focus and the answers will come to you I promise.

My Thomas the tank, I am so proud of the gentle giant that you have become. You are to say the least, the one that has always know what he has wanted and gone for it. You are extremely smart, have an amazing outlook on life and you will become everything you know you will be.

Libbie Loopy, ,my best friend, from the day you were born, you have radiated that light you have within you all along. You shine so bright that the rest of the world will benefit from the LOVE you have in your heart one day. Remember to always keep shining as bright as the star that you are, this world needs more people like you so it can heal from the cruelty that had been bestowed upon it, I have faith that you will, one day become the woman that I have always known you would be.

My Simon, my partner in crime, my little man, you are to say the least one of the most unique little boys I have ever had the opportunity to know. You have and will always have that special place in my heart, where you have touched my soul like no other. You can and will become to be a young man one day and offer this world one of the most important things it needs, and that is YOU, just keep being who you are, true, authentic, loveable and just amazing keep shining bright my little man.

The one and only Rhiannon, you are the one person I can say that has always been that diamond in my life that has always been there, you have and can be the one that will always make it to where you need to be. You have the strength inside you like no other, you have gone through life with an open heart, you see the good in everyone you meet, that LOVE you have inside of you is just phenomenal. You have a great husband and have given me three absolutely beautiful grandchildren, I know I wasn't the one that gave birth to you, but you will always be my daughter. I Love you will all of my heart and more.

Kye, I would like to say thank you for being the one that is going to be there throughout my sons life. You are a beautiful, talented, spectacular young lady. Like I said to

Lee-Andrew, go within and seek that one thing you have always been searching for, it is within you, and has been all along, you need to find what it is you have been searching for. The answers will come to you, and you will become the happiest you have ever been, you just need to look within yourself to find it. I LOVE you loads and never forget that.

To all the people that has come into my life, good and bad, I would like to say a huge thank you for teaching me what it was I needed to know, to be able to go forward on my journey and find the real me. You have taught me what not to let into my life, and what it was I needed in it, if it wasn't for all of you people, life wouldn't be what it is today.

Make life count, never look back, always keep looking forward, as life gives and takes away, but remember it only gives you what you need and will take away anything that doesn't serve you. If it's not meant to be in your life it wont be, if it is then it will be there for as long as you need it to be.

Take this as you will, take what you need and leave what you don't for anyone else that may, find that peace of the missing puzzle, your heart will guide you to where it needs to be.

LOVE and LIGHT, until we meet again, I LOVE you all.
Julie Watts.

Acknowledgements

OUT OF THE DARK AND INTO THE LIGHT.

ACKNOWLEDGEMENTS.

I would like to give praise to several people who have been a huge part of my life, firstly I would like to say thank you to the BIG man himself for always being there when I needed him. I would also like to say thank you to my divine team (my spirit guides), for always listening and answering me every time I have asked them for help. I wasn't aware of my divine team (spirit guides) when I was a child, or for the best part of my adult life, but back in the year, 2021, something inside me changed for the better, and I started to talk to my spirit guides, and without hesitation they always answered me.

Growing up I always knew I was different from most, if not all, people that were in or entered my life, when I say different, I mean not fitting in to society that has been set out for the world by people of this world who seem to think they know what's best for all humankind. I was never the popular girl in school, (when I was in school that is), and the other children just didn't seem to understand me, which followed me all through my adult life. I left school at the age of fourteen, as the stuff they were teaching me just wasn't sinking in, I always felt different, and now at the age of forty four I know, I am different, which is not a bad thing, in fact its amazing, to be different I know love who I am and look forward to enjoying the rest of my journey on this beautiful place we call planet earth.

I would love to say a huge thank you to all those people that stood by me when times were tough and unbearable, when I hit my all-time lows "as there were quite a few", and helped me get back to being the kind hearted loving person I knew I always was. But there isn't anyone to thank, ,except MYSELF Julie Ann Watts, me, the only one that stood by me and talked me through all the bad times and brought me back to being the person I always knew I was, but forgot for a while along the way here.

To the ancestors that has watched over me from birth, and the ones I've lost along the way, thank you for guiding me and continue to guide me through my journey on this planet. One more thank you to the light that has guided me through the best

Chapter 1 The Beginning.

CHAPTER ONE: THE BEGINNING.

Let me introduce myself, my name is Julie, and I am 44 years old as of today. Back in 2021 my life changed for the better, like a lot of people I started having my spiritual awakening. Ever since I was younger, I always felt like I was the odd one out, I didn't fit in any where no one excepted me, friends were few and family, well let's just say that it wasn't your normal family life for me.

I lived with my both parents up until I was about two when they separated and there was just mum myself and my older brother, as I found out later on in life, my farther preferred to date the same sex, which of cause is fine but my farther decide to hide this from the rest of the world as it just wasn't excepted in the gypsy culture, so he went on to live his life hiding from who he really was, which must have been extremally hard for him never being able to truly be who he felt he was inside. No one should ever be made to feel that way. My farther decided to move far away from where myself and brother were living with mum which made visitation very little.

I don't recall much of my life before the age of seven as I think I've decided to block most of it out due to things that had happened in my family home. Mum was in her twenty's when she separated from my farther, that's when life for my mum myself and my brother became what it was to become. At the age of seven my mother decided to send my brother to stay with my farther for a couple of weeks as she said he was misbehaving, and she needed him to help with him. After my brother was sent to stay with my farther all I remember from then until eight years after that is a few visits with my farther while my brother came to visit my mother because those two weeks turned into eight years.

There were two stories of why my brother ended up staying with my farther and never returning to live with me and mum, well I say two stories, there were three, my father's my mothers and of cause the truth. My father's version was that my mother never wanted him back as he was to uncontrollable and then my mother's side of the story which she claimed my farther had moved address and decided not to let her know where they were living, then there's the third side of the story, the true side that is only known between my mother and my farther.

During the eight years of little visits and any kind of contact with my father and brother, life for me living with my mother became extremely difficult. It was hard enough for me being apart from my brother and farther and having to cope with feeling different from the rest of the kids my age, life was lonely, mum went off into her own little world of alcohol and prostitsion.

Affirmations.

I release control of the things I cannot accept.

Instead of forcing things to go a certain way,

I trust the universe is working on my behalf.

I see that everything in life has its own time and place,

And I allow all to be as it is.

Chapter 2 The Child Who Was Forgotten

CHAPTER TWO: THE CHILD WHO WAS FORGOTTEN.

Looking back at my life now I don't know if any other family members knew about mum prostituting, or if they just decided to turn a blind eye and let her live her own life, as life for them was hard enough without having to deal with my mother and the way in which she decides to live hers. Growing up without a farther figure in my life when mum brought home a man that lasted longer than a few months, I clung to them like there was no tomorrow, other family members just looked at me like there was something wrong with me and that it was unhealthy for me to doing what I was doing. But I was lonely and needed someone, someone that understood me, someone that was going to stay longer than a few months, but it never happened no matter how tight I clung to them, they always left in the end.

Mum liked to drink a lot, first it was just in the evenings or when a man or two would visit her, but then it became as early as teatime. Back then she liked to drink wine, I always remember a box of wine on the side and whisky when her man friends would visit, the men would always water theirs down while mum drank hers straight, then I would be sent to bed while they continued to drink and be loud downstairs. Most nights when the men would visit her, I was always woken up early hours in the morning to the noise of my mum and what ever man she had over that night having sex in the room next door. One night I remember waking up to this strange man hovering over me and my mother telling him that he had to leave me alone now and to leave the money under my pillow, I remember the man saying (but I love her), I don't ever recall seeing that man before or ever again. I guess I must have drifted back off to sleep as I don't remember anything else about that night, not even the money that was left under my pillow, maybe I just blocked it out because of what I would have remembered, probably one of the best decisions I ever made.

There were so many times when my mother would get that drunk she wouldn't even be able to make it up the stairs without falling, this one time when I was seven I remember her saying it was time for bed and we both went to go up at the same time, but as she took her first two steps up the stairs she fell backwards hitting her head on the wall and passing out, she started to vomit while upside down and passed out as I was only seven I didn't know what to do so as I was just about to walk out the front door to see if I could find someone to help she came around got up and said (come on time for bed). I told her what had just happened, and she giggled to herself and went on up the stairs to bed. The next couple of days after this happened, my mum just shrugged it off as if it was normal and laughed about it with everyone, she spoke to or saw.

Affirmations.

I step forward with confidence and trust my new beginning is appropriate for my big picture.

My life is important and I allow myself to be fully in the process.

It is safe to release all troubling situations.

Chapter 3 Tough Times

CHAPTER THREE: TOUGH TIMES.

Life got harder, mum drank even more, she also had different men in and out of our lives, she even started going out leaving me home alone sometimes for days and no one seemed to think that this was a problem. After this going on for years without anyone taking any notice of how this was affecting me, life just seemed even more lonely, that's when I started going out more myself and hanging out with kids and even adults that were defiantly not good for me to be around.

At the age of eleven my mother took me to social services, as she said my behaviour had gotten out of control and needed help with me. As we were leaving social service that day my mother told me I wasn't allowed out when we got home so I told her I wasn't going home with her then. That day she left me with social service and told them she couldn't cope and for them to do what they could with me. that night I was sent to a foster home. I don't think I was bothered about being sent there, I was quite excited to go, anything was better than going home with my mother. I was at the foster home for about one week, they were lovely people and the house I was staying in wasn't to far from where I lived, so I was still able to go and visit my friends. I didn't go visit my mother whilst I went to visit my friends even though she was only in the next street over, I didn't want to see her.

My mother and her side of the family just labelled me as a spoilt little brat that stomped her feet when she couldn't get her own way. I was far from spoilt, if I remember correctly, I didn't have much as a child, I never had the latest clothes like all the other kids my age, my mother would shop in the charity shops and by me what the cheapest of what they had for sale in there. Don't get me wrong I absolutely love charity shops now, in fact I don't shop anywhere else unless I must, but back when I was a child the items my mother bought for me, well let's just say I defiantly didn't fit in with the rest of the children my age.

Affirmations.

All of my needs are met, I am full of LOVE and my attention is on the present moment.

No matter what the outcome,

I know it will be for my greater good.

Chapter 4 The Rebelling Stage.

CHAPTER FOUR: THE REBELLING STAGE.

I started smoking at the age of eleven, sealing from my mother and any man that would come over, I would wait until she took them upstairs and go down stairs go through their pockets and take money from their wallets, I was hoping that if I did this they wouldn't come back but they always did no matter how many times I did it they just started taking their wallets up stairs with them. They knew it was me taking their money but when my mother confronted me about it, I would just say it wasn't me. I would get grounded for a few days that was about all my mother could take of me being around her, I hated being grounded I just wanted to be away from my mother so when I did get grounded I would shout, stomp me feet at the top of the stairs and anything else I could think of that would annoy her so she would get sick of me and send me out to get away from her.

At the age of twelve, I remember being out with my friends, we were hanging out in a block of flats when this boy (his name was Jamie Davis) came up to me and said hello, before he could say anything else I just looked at him and said I would go get my friend for him now, as I turned to walk away he grabbed my arm and said that it was me he wanted to talk to not my friend, I think I must of stood there for a good few minutes with my mouth open not knowing what to say before he asked me to go for a walk with him. That first kiss was amazing it was my first kiss, I still remember how it made me feel to this day. We started dating and hanging out nearly every night he was fifteen I was twelve, he reminded me of the boy out the band (new kids on the block) Mark Wallberk, he was hot, and I was his girlfriend, life seemed good for the first time ever.

We had been dating for a couple of months, on valentine's day he came to mine and my mother had let him in my room with me, we were kissing and cuddling on my bed when he started to touch me, I got very uncomfortable and asked him to leave, he did leave and that was it we were over as I just didn't know how to deal with those feelings I was having, they were feelings I had never experienced before and just didn't know what to do about them, so I did nothing and just never spoke to him again. I often wondered how life turned out for him not sure why, but I guess looking back now he was my first love, I just didn't know it at the time. Not ever experiencing those kinds of feelings ever, there was no way I would have known that it was love.

I didn't date anyone for a while after Jamie, I think I had a few crushes, but I never did anything about them. I just spent most of my time either in my room or out with my friends, hanging around the streets smoking and getting up to anything we shouldn't have been getting up to.

Affirmations.

Set backs in life can be surprising opportunities for growth.

Although this time of my life may be uncertain,

I trust my future self is guiding me.

I am willing to see the silver lining and am open to living my life in refreshing new ways.

Chapter 5 Adulthood to Early.

CHAPTER FIVE: ADULTHOOD TO EARLY.

At the age of thirteen I started going to night clubs with my friends, that's when I got the taste for alcohol. Me and my one friend that I had been friends with since I was four would get dressed up in our long patchwork hippy skirts that reached all the way down to our ankles, with our miniskirts underneath so we could change when we got to where we were going. My mother didn't care what I wore out, but my friend's mother did, so I wouldn't just go along with what was best for my friend, so no questions were asked. Some nights we wouldn't even make it home, we would just stay wherever everyone was going that night then go straight back to the pub the next morning, all this was happening from the age of thirteen to the age of sixteen.

We would go out every weekend, we would leave early afternoon go out drinking, sniffing gas and whatever else was on offer, it got so bad for me that from the top to the bottom of the underneath of my mattress was full of aerosol cans, any think from lighter gas to hair spray cans to deodorant cans, all empty, I was sniffing anything I could get my hands on, this all came to an end when my mother found them underneath my mattress. I never did out of the dark into the light

sniff gas or any kind of aerosol ever again.

Affirmations.

I don't always get what I want but I know I will always get
what I truly need.

I may feel stuck and at a standstill at times,

But when I turn inward I know all is in order.

I know I am being guided.

Chapter 6 The Unknown.

CHAPTER SIX: THE UNKNOWN.

After three years of constant drinking, sniffing gas and partying where and when ever I could, two months after I turned sixteen, I went to this heavy metal club with my friend, that's when I met the man, I would spend the next twenty eights' years of my life with. I remember the night as if it was yesterday, we were out at the club when this man, (which I had met before when I was fifteen), he bought me a drink, then asked me how old I was, when I told him I was fifteen he was like "oh that's to young", left to be with another girl. But that night when he came to sit next to me and asked (how old are you now) I told him I was sixteen thinking he would just say the same thing he said last time he asked me my age, but this time he didn't, instead he said (that's old enough) and we kissed.

At the end of that night when it was time to go home, me and my friend left the club and went the opposite direction to which the man I was going to spend the next twenty-eight years with went. The club was only a short walk to my house, as we got halfway home, we heard voices shouting from behind us, it was him, the man from the club with his friend, he had followed us (well that's what we thought at the time) he just said he was going that way. He was a lot older than I was as I had just turned sixteen and he was twenty-four turning twenty-five two months after we met.

Affirmations.

I am in the journey of my life and I embrace each moment fully.

Each difficult experience is a pathway to greatness within me.

All setbacks are really growth and part of my overarching plan.

Chapter 7 Devastation.

CHAPTER SEVEN: DEVASTATION.

Just after meeting him, it was roughly about four months when my mother had been rushed into hospital with blood clots on the brain, me being sixteen and none the wiser of how serious this was, I just took it as it came, she spent six months in hospital, after three brain operations and endless amounts of medication before finding the right one for her she came home. Two weeks after she got out of hospital, I was cleaning the house to help her out when I found a black bag full of empty cider bottles that her and her new alcoholic boyfriend had consumed within those two weeks. He was probably one of the nicest boyfriends she had ever been with as he really did care for her, but him being an alcoholic too was just a disaster waiting to happen. Their relationship lasted a few years, one of the longest she had ever had since splitting from my farther.

After my mother's brain surgery her drinking became extreme, where she would replace her morning coffee with a glass of cider. She never did come to terms with what had happened to her, she was never offered any counselling after it, and with her being the way she was, a person that never new how to love or except love because of the up bringing she had gone through this just through her over the edge, she took to drinking even more to cover up all those emotions that needed dealing with.

During all this that was going on with my mother I was just starting my new relationship with my boyfriend, as he was a lot older than me, he knew how serious my mother's surgery was, as I was still none the wiser, even though everyone kept telling me how serious it was it just wouldn't sink in. Nothing like this had ever happen in my family or to anyone I new before and it wasn't until years later I realised how serious it was, it probably wasn't until my mother passed away from an enridge behind the eye, I finally realised it was serious.

It was a good three months before mine and my boyfriend's relationship became physical, I had only been in one physical relationship with one other person before him (well if you can call it that) being the age I am now I wouldn't called it a physical relationship. The first few months were great, he was lovely to me, he would take me out with him, we spent nearly every day together, which is what you want when you start dating someone, if he wasn't down my house, I would be up his where he lived with his mum stepdad, stepbrother, and sister. A few months after we started dating round about the time when our relationship had become physical, that's when things started to change, not at a great rate but changed all the same.

Affirmations.

I am connected to my true self and know all is in perfect order.

I have goals and deep desires, but they will be manifested in their own right time and place.

I release my need to have things when and how I want,

And I turn my trust to the universe.

I always get what I need when I need it,

I surrender.

Chapter 8 Changing.

CHAPTER EIGHT: CHANGING.

My boyfriend would go out with his friends, he wouldn't invite me along, there was one friend he had, that when he did go out with him, he would take me along, but that's just because his friend had his girlfriend with him all the time. They lived just around the conner from my mother's house, I became friends with his girlfriend, we would all go out for a drive, up the forest and get drunk and stoned, we had a laugh.

A few weeks after introducing me to his friends girlfriend I went around to visit her without him, and she was home with one of their other friends, we were all sat around talking when suddenly out of nowhere he was there my boyfriend, with this look of disgust on his face asking me what I was doing there, he started shouting because there was a man there, he told me to get out of there so I got up, when I started to walk down the stairs he started pushing me nearly making me fall, as we got outside, he told me to get in the car so I did. I wasn't sure what was going on because this was the first time, I had saw him this way. I can't remember exactly what was said in the car ride that day but what I do remember is that was the beginning of him controlling me.

That day of him nearly pushing me down the stairs, his friend's girlfriend had gone over the road to let my mum know what had happened, by the time we got back after the car ride there was about five people there waiting to confront him about what he had done. Me being young and thinking that he did what he did because he loved me, took his side over my mums, I ended up getting kicked out that night having to move into boyfriend's mother's house with him.

I was seventeen at the time of moving into his mother's house with him. We lived in his mother's house for about two months before moving into our own flat together, this was the first time ever not living with my mum. We moved into the flat with just our clothes and a few bits and bobs, we didn't have a washing machine at the time, I had to wash his oily work clothes by hand, but not knowing any better as I was never taught by anyone how life and relationships were supposed to be I thought this was normal.

Affirmations.

I except my path and growth through all challenges with a determination to succeed.

The universe is supporting me, and I will soar.

My path becomes clear as I take more steps forward.

I am confident and sure of myself.

Chapter 9 Abuse.

CHAPTER NINE: ABUSE.

In our first flat is the first time he ever put his hands on me, I don't remember what or why it happened, but he got that angry he dragged me from one end of the room to the other, it was only because his sister was screaming at him to leave me alone that he stopped otherwise I don't know what might have happened. I know I was young and probably a right pain in the ass at times, but he was nine years older than I was and had done this sort of stuff before in his previous relationships, whatever I did that day he shouldn't of never of put his hands on me, he should have been old and wise enough to be able to walk away from whatever it was I did to piss him off.

I was young and didn't know any better, I wasn't perfect, I didn't have a clue how a relationship worked so I just went with the way things were. I was young, annoying, clingy, and probably a right pain in the ass, I thought that it was all my fault he treated me the way he did. The hair pulling happened a few times while we were living in the flat, but if I did things the way he wanted them done things were ok. While we were still living in the flat his friend's girlfriend had started seeing one of his other friends, she became pregnant with his baby, about one month into her pregnancy his friend had a bad accident and passed away.

My boyfriend took it upon himself be the one that was going to be there for his friend's pregnant girlfriend.

 I was eighteen when all this was going on, it went on for about eight months, where he would come home from work and go straight to see her saying she needed him while making sure at the same time I wasn't going anywhere, making sure I spent most of my time at the flat, making up all sorts of excuses for me not to go out, he spent that much time with this girl that when he finally did take me to the pub with him they thought she was his girlfriend and asked where she was and what he was doing with me. He just laughed it off as if it was a joke, not even realising it was me he was making to look and feel like the joke.

After spending a few years in the flat we moved into a two-bedroom house, that's when I became pregnant with my first son, (my BABA). Before me and my boyfriend met, he had just come back from America, he went to live there when he was twelve to go live with his dad when his parents split. While he was there, he had three daughters, he married the last woman he had a child with, so when we met, he was still married and took him the best part of seventeen years after we got together to get a divorce from her. This was the reason he would say we couldn't get married.

After moving into the new house my boyfriend was still spending a lot of time with this girl, he thought he had to look after her because she was pregnant with his friend's baby who had passed away. He would cause arguments with me just so he could go off and see her, he spent that much time with her that it was me that was feeling like the other woman in his life. The one day he had asked me to go pick up something from a friend's house for him, that was the day I got told by his friend and his friend's girlfriend that he was there a few weeks ago saying he was in love with this pregnant girl but didn't want to get rid of me. Of cause he denied everything and the girl in question didn't seem to know what I was on about when I asked her.

Thinking back, I now realise that he was in love with that girl, I remember the way he used to look at her, the way he treated her, he never did look at treat me the same way he did her, not once in the twenty-eight years of us being together did he ever look at me the way he looked at her.

Affirmations.

I am connected to my emotions and I feel them fully.

Any area of my life that feels painful is an opportunity to go inward.

I reflect on my pian and see what needs to be changed.

Chapter 10 Time to Leave.

CHAPTER TEN: TIME TO LEAVE.

 We lived in the two-bedroom house for about two years, before after numerous times of me leaving and going back, I found out he had been cheating on me, so I left to go live back with my mum and took our son with me. There were times that he would punch me in the back of the head while I was holding my son when he was only a few months old, then would say that I couldn't prove that he had hit me as there wasn't ant marks on me. I went from being very quiet and cowering in the corner when he would shout at me, to answering him back, as now I had to protect my son, becoming a mother changed me as it does most people, I became stronger and wiser to the way he behaved.

I lived with my mother for a couple of months, there were times when he would come around and bang on the door, causing a scene outside my mums, one time someone called the police on him but when they came and asked his name they said they new him and that he was a lovely man, which made me feel like it was me that had something wrong with them. No one saw him for who he truly was, everyone liked him, and he was only that way with me, he only showed his true colours in front of a select few. Three weeks before I was ready to move into my own place with our son, he, worked his way back into our lives, we ended up moving into the new house together.

Affirmations.

My life is in perfect balance because I take care of myself and follow my heart.

I honour my needs.

I allow myself to be recognized and I embrace the power of the pause.

Chapter 11 Life Changing Moment

CHAPTER ELEVEN: LIFE CHANGING MOMENT.

We were only at the new house for about a year and a half when things started to go bad between us, he was a taxi driver at the time, worked nights and slept all day until he got back up for work. One Sunday on the sixth of February the year 2000, I got his phone call, it was dinner time I remember as I was just finishing making a Sunday roast when the phone rang, it was my mothers boyfriend on the other end, saying he couldn't wake my mother up and that I needed to go there, me being used to my mum drinking to much said just give a good shake and put the phone down. About five minutes later the phone rang again, this time it was my mother's boss, he said (I don't know what your mother's boyfriend just told you, but the ambulance men are there now trying to revive her). Not sure what I had just heard, my boyfriend phoned for a taxi, I left to go to my mothers. When I arrived the police and an ambulance were there, as I walked into her flat, I went straight into her bedroom, there she was lying on the floor with her sister sitting over her crying her eyes out.

Not quite taking anything in, I walked into the living room where her boyfriend, boss and the police were, for some unknown reason her boyfriend couldn't speak English (even though all the time he was with my mother he could speak perfect English) the police told me they had to get an interpreter to speak with him at the police station. I never did find out what exactly happened after the police took him away, but I do know no charges were ever made against him. My mums boss told me that when he came to my mums that day she passed, her boyfriend had taken a knife from underneath the sofa and put it back in the kitchen, he told the police this but like I said no charges were ever brought against him. The cause of death was a blood clot behind the eye.

My mother the young age of forty-eight when she passed away, four days after her birthday, I was twenty-one. I don't think I ever did grieve for my mum as I never felt she had ever really gone, it always felt like she's been there, I mean I've cried and thought about all the things we never got to experience together, and the fact she never got to meet my other three children. It was just an ache in my heart that got added to the rest of the aches that sit there with room for many aches to come. And they came, day by day month by month and year by year they all added up. When people would pass away, I would look at the other people's reactions to losing their loved ones, I couldn't understand why I never felt that way, I always thought there was something wrong with me, that I had just become cold hearted, and nothing seemed to bother me in the same way as it did other people.

Affirmations.

What once bothered me no longer affects me,

For I am peace and harmony.

I can be calm in the chaos because I am a beacon of
LOVE and LIGHT.

Chapter 12 Blame.

CHAPTER TWELVE: BLAME.

The day before she passed away, she phoned me and told me that she had this bad headache and asked me if she should phone the doctors or just go out for the night she had planned already. I told her to just go out, that she will be fine. For years I blamed myself for not telling her to phone the doctors, because if she had she might still be here today. Now I know it was just her time to go, we all have that set date when its time for us to part from this place we call earth, and that was her time.

Affirmations.

I am hopeful in all areas of my life.

I am aligned with my truth, which is LOVE.

I turn my fears over to the universe.

LOVE will guide me home.

Chapter 13 The Beginning of the End.

CHAPTER THIRTEEN: THE BEGINNING OF THE END.

After my mother had passed things between me and my boyfriend just got worse. It was four months after she had passed away when I remember he got up for work, he had asked me to go around to the phone box (as we didn't have mobile phones back then or couldn't afford a house phone), but because I refused to as it just would have been easier for him to go himself, he got so angry he got my mother's jewellery box grabbed the hammer and smashed it up right there Infront of me. Things went from bad to worse, he was gambling most of his wages and what he wasn't gambling he was spending on his coke habit as well as cheating on me.

I couldn't take anymore of the way things were I never had any money and the money he was earning for his job he was using for his gambling and drug habit; I asked him to leave. He did leave that day in fact he couldn't wait to leave; he went to stay with his mum. We were separated for about four months; in that time, I had found out he was sleeping with eight different women and took it upon himself to set fire to the house after moving all his belongings out. Due to the house being set on fire, and with him getting away with it, I had to move in with my auntie with my son. Our son was four at the time and the most adorable blond haired blue eyed little boy you had ever seen (that's my opinion) I wasn't the only one going through everything I was going through; my little boy was witnessing all this too. We stayed with my auntie for about six months before getting our own place, times were so hard for both of us I was having to do everything myself for the first time ever without my mother being there to help and my little boy was experiencing it with me.

Affirmations.

I am not attached to the outcome of situations in my life.

I feel connected to my purpose and see how everything works together.

I see that there is no such thing as a setback.

I am always being nudged into a new awareness of self and I am connected to my life and I focus forward with LOVE.

Chapter 14 Watching and Waiting.

CHAPTER FOURTEEN: WATCHING AND WAITING.

After moving into our new home with the help of my aunties and uncles, we did have much just a few items I managed to salvage from the fire and whatever my family could help me out with. The first couple of weeks were the hardest but we managed. I managed to put some money away to buy the paint I needed to start my son's bedroom, I wanted him to have his own room after everything he had been through, I thought it was the best place to start when it came to decorating the new house.

I remember the day I was painting my son's bedroom, I could sense someone watching me, as I turned to look out the window, there he was sitting in his car watching me, I panicked and just left the room. A few days had past when a friend of mine told me that my ex-boyfriend at the time, had phoned her to say his daughter was coming over from America, he wanted our BABA to meet her, me being me, agreed for this to happen. He picked us up in his car and went for a drive, on this drive he told me he had something he needed to tell me, that's the day he told me he had cheated on me and had another child with someone else, a daughter, she was two weeks old at the time he was telling me this. We worked through things and we got back together. The day after we got back together, he got a phone call from his baby's mother asking him if he was having her that day, he looked at me, I just told him that it was his decision to make not mine, once he had made his decision, then I would decide if I could deal with it or not.

 Looking back now I feel that I made that decision for him by saying what I had said that day, he decided he wasn't going to see his daughter. If it had been today all this was happening things would have been different and I would have made the decision for him to see his daughter, as that day he made the decision not to see her because of the answer I gave him affected that little girl's life forever. Being someone who never had their father around when she was growing up, and it affecting me the way it did, I should never have allowed that to happen to another little girl. Even though she never had him in her life for the best part of eleven years, she had a good home life and became the amazing young lady she is today, beautiful, extremally talented and has a good heart, she could of easily of gone the opposite way.

Getting back together after being apart for four months, life was never going to be the same again, not like it used to be, things had change even if I was the only one that was going to grow from the experiences that had happened in our relationship. Some people use the experiences they have in their life as an excuse to be bitter at the world and everyone that has or had caused them any sort of pain.

Affirmations.

I release all expectations and allow myself to be in the flow of life.

I embrace the journey and let things unfold naturally.

The situations I am in are part of my life plan.

I except them as though I had chosen them myself.

I release all expectations and trust that things are as they should be.

Chapter 15 Learning.

CHAPTER FIFTHTEEN: LEARNING.

 Letting go is not an option for some people, holding on to the pain and anger toughens their heart and causes them to hate, holding on to anger will never solve anything, letting go and learning to forgive whatever it was that caused you that pain which made you feel bitter towards the world is the only way you are ever going to heal yourself.

Being twenty-one, mother to a four-year-old little boy and in a toxic relationship took its toll on me. My little boy was on the verge of getting kicked out of school because he was hitting out at the teachers, me and his farther were arguing almost all the time about things that had happened when we were apart, we were drinking, taking drugs and partying almost every weekend. I didn't have many friends as that the way I liked it, but I became friends with this one girl that had lived a few doors away, she was nice, I liked her, she also had a little boy who was just a little younger than my son. My boyfriend wasn't that sure about her as he had heard people talking about her and her antics with men. This did not sit well with him at all he told me that I was to stop speaking to her, I refused, and we had gotten into another argument about it, but this argument became more serious than any one we had ever had before. We were at the top of the stairs when all this was going on, because I wasn't agreeing to his demands about not speaking to the girl a few doors down he smashed my head into the door frame, things went blurry, I felt something dripping down the side of my face. As I turned to look at him, he had this look on his face, like he became very concerned about me suddenly. He became very caring towards me trying to see where the blood was coming from, he said something along the lines like (what did you do, why did you walk into the door frame), his friend which witness everything shouted something up the stairs and left the house, the look on his face said everything, he knew exactly what had happened.

That night I went to the hospital, they told me I had to have my head glued, they asked me what had happened, I told them exactly what he said that I had walked into to door frame trying to leave an argument with my boyfriend. The doctors knew what had happened but what could they do if I wasn't willing to tell the truth they just had to take what I was saying as what happened.

Affirmations.

Starting now, I focus forward.

I align my energy with LOVE and support.

I let go of my past, for today is the only day that matters.

What I do today has the potential to improve all my tomorrows.

Chapter 16 Seeing their True Colours.

CHAPTER SIXTEEN: SEEING THEIR TRUE COLOURS.

Five years we lived in the apartment, and it was not easy, everyday just seemed to be a challenge, from people being over all the time, girls flirting with my boyfriend and him thinking it was ok. There was this one girl who moved in with her little boy she used to visit mine and I would hers, he didn't seem to mind her she was quiet and kept herself to herself. He knew her and her family from when he was a taxi driver. Her little boy was about four at the time she moved in, and we had been there nearly five years, it was just the two of them and when I asked her about the father, she just said that he didn't want to know him and that was all that was said about it.

Later I discovered that when me and my boyfriend had split up, he was with this girl, and I often wondered if that little boy was his as he looked just like my son when he was his age. She was such a quiet lovely girl, I believe that if the boy was my boyfriends, and he had told her that he didn't want anything to do with him, because of being with me and what it would do to our relationship, that she would agree with anything thing he would have asked her. If you had met her, you would understand why I am saying that about her. She just wasn't the type of girl that would have done anything to break up another relationship.

I was twenty-five when I fell pregnant with our second son "Thomas the tank", I gave him his nickname because he was built like a tank, he was such a hungry baby that we started feeding him solid food at the age a one and a halve months old. When he got to the age of about four months, he would chew on the bone of a spear rib and suck on a corn on the cob without the corn on it, he loved his food and still does to this day and yes still my Thomas the tank.

 Things never got any better between me and my boyfriend, still the same arguing about the same stuff, (same shit different day), still partying, taking drugs smoking weed, it got to the point where I was that depressed, I went to the doctors, they gave me tablets for my depression. They did help a little, well they covered up my feelings, so I didn't have to deal with them because that's all they do, is sugar coat what is really going on inside, they don't solve the problem. The problem wasn't the fact I was depressed it was in fact I just hadn't found myself yet and covering up my feelings was never going to help me find who I truly was, you need to feel, you need to cry, you need to think about everything that has gone on in your life to be able to heal.

Letter to my younger self.

Dear Julie

I am writing you this letter from the future, I know this may sound crazy, but I really need to talk to you, it's important.

I just want to let you know how much I LOVE you, and that everything will be ok in the future.

You're going to go through some extremally hard times in

your life, and I mean hard. Your strong so you will be fine, it is all happening to you to prepare you for when the time is right. When everything you have gone through will make sense to you, it will make sense I promise. Just remember to always be yourself, never change for anyone and I mean anyone. You're going to be a pain in the ass until you get to an age when you start to understand life a little better. This is only because you are seeking attention from the people that are supposed to LOVE you. You're not a bad girl.

When you reach the age of sixteen, you will meet this man, this is when life really does get tough. There will be times when you feel like ending your life, but you don't, you're a fighter, a warrior, you chose this life before you were born. Every punch, every hair pulls, all the heart ache, the mental pain, this happens to you to make you the strongest you can be, and you will be, you're the strongest person I know.

Nothing can destroy you and I mean nothing. Keep LOVING with all your heart, that's all you'll ever need, just keep LOVING and never stop. One day that LOVE will be returned to you tenfold I promise you this. KEEP SMILING LOVE YOU ALWAYS.

Chapter 17 Embarrassing Moment.

CHAPTER SEVENTEEN: EMBARRASSING MOMENT.

Life seemed to be going ok, I had two amazing little boys, well not so little but amazing nevertheless, my boyfriend was coaching my son football team, so he was somewhat happy about himself. He loved football watching and paling it, so to be a coach of something he loved really kept him busy. As my boyfriend was now the coach of my son's football team, there was a football tour coming up for the boys and we were invited to attend. It was a week away with a lot of people from a few of the football teams from the same town. There was me my two sons my boyfriend and we also took his brother with us. We were a few days into the tour when I told my boyfriend that I didn't want to go back to the after party they were having for a drink because I just knew, I could tell that they really didn't like him, I felt uncomfortable being around them. But my boyfriend being the way he was, just said that there was something wrong with me, that I never like to be around other people and he was just going to go without me, which I didn't mind if I didn't have to be there. I believe it was about one in the morning when he came back to the place we were staying and told me, he thinks the police were coming to arrest him, when I asked him why he said because he punched this lady in the face, when he told me this, he had this huge grin on his face like he had done something good. The police did come, and he did get arrested that night.

The day after. So now I was miles away from home couldn't drive at the time, two young boys and a baby to look after whilst at the same time the rest of the team members looking at me in disgust because of what my boyfriend had done. I packed our stuff and filled the car not knowing what to do or who to contact about my boyfriend, so I ended up phoning a friend to come and pick us up. By the time our friend turned up, my boyfriend got released dew to the fact that someone had witnessed the whole thing and it was self-defence, he got let off. Even if it was self-defence that sort of behaviour is just not acceptable, it was an embarrassment to myself and to my oldest son, who got tormented by the lady's son in school for such a long time afterwards. But to him it was just another experience in his life that he could talk and laugh about to everyone and anyone. But it wasn't the story he was telling that bothered me it was the way in which he would tell it, like he was a big man for doing what he had done, he thought it made him look cool.

Chapter 18 Nothing prepares you for Life.

CHAPTER EIGHTTEEN: NOTHING PREPARES YOU FOR LIFE.

Life never prepares you for anything, it doesn't come with a handbook and even if you have an amazing childhood there is always a chance you're not going to be prepared for adult life. They say you choose the life you're going to have before you are born, and I deeply believe this, but not until I got to the age, I am now. I've always been a day dreamer believing in something bigger than what this world has to offer, I didn't know what it was back when I was a child or most of my adult life, but now I know that all those times I would look up and say whatever it was I was saying or asking for would one day be answered. If only they taught children in school all about the things people are starting to discover in today's society.

Round about October 2005 I fell pregnant with our third child, she was born in the July 2006, my beautiful baby girl Libbie Loopy, this is the nick name I gave to her when she was around one and a half, as she was just the loopiest little girl I had ever known, she was so independent. When she got to the age of twelve months old, she would keep taking her nappy off, she just wanted to be a big girl and there was no stopping her. When she ran her top part of her body would always seem like it was way in front of her legs, she couldn't even keep up with herself, she has grown to be a beautiful young lady, with enormous amounts of talent, (even if she doesn't recognise it yet), she is amazing and my best friend anyone would be proud to have her as theirs too.

When Libbie was born, she was born with a full head of black hair, not like my two sons. My eldest son Lee – Andrew was born with blond hair like me and my boyfriend, then there's Thomas my second son he was born with ginger hair like his grand parents on my side of the family and my boyfriend's side. So, when Libbie was born with a full head of black hair, the day after she was born my boyfriend asked me if she was even his. Women everywhere who has had children will tell you that your emotions are everywhere after giving birth, so to be questioned with something like this was just awful. A few months later Libbie's hair started to change to blond, that's when I wasn't questioned about it ever again, not sure if her hair had stayed black, he might have still questioned the fact if she was his still to this day.

The year 2006, the week before Libbie was born, I had passed my driving test on the Friday moved house on the Sunday, then the Friday after that I gave birth to my baby girl. The house was upside down as we had only just moved in. We were all sleeping in one bedroom on a couple of mattresses, while we decorated the rest of the house. For the next couple of years life went on as normal. As I was now a mother to three amazing children the drinking and drugs was non-existent in my home, my boyfriend smoked cannabis, but no other drug was ever taken after we had our third child, in fact if I remember correctly, it was after I gave birth to Thomas for me the drinking and drug taking stopped completely, I was totally coffee only.

Chapter 19 Taking it all in.

CHAPTER NINETEEN: TAKING IT ALL IN.

For years after, the weekend partying continued, but for me I still didn't drink, I just sat back and watch the rest of the party get totally out of control. This went on for about two and a half years, me not drinking, but one day I thought to myself if everyone else is drinking I guess it won't hurt if I have a drink, so I decided to get involved with the rest of the party, I was always the one who was left out of everything because I didn't drink, so I started again.

Living with my boyfriend was not an easy thing to do, he was controlling, moody, and I'd say that he probably has about at least five different personalities and that's me being nice. I found myself drinking more and more every day till it got to the point I couldn't go a day without having a drink, it wasn't just one or two bottles of beers a day it was a few glasses of vodka a day. As the fighting continued on a weekly basis, the more the different personality's continued to surface the more I just wanted to drink to numb myself, I wasn't happy in any area of my life the only thing that was right in my life was my children, but this didn't stop me from wanting to just disappear from the nightmare I was living.

Chapter 20 Never to be the same again.

CHAPER TWENTY: NEVER TO BE THE SAME AGAIN.

Life continued as if nothing was wrong. In September 2009 we had decided to go out as a family, we took the kids to the zoo for the day, it was quite a drive there, but we all had a lovely time. As we were loading up the car to go home, (I remember it as if it was yesterday) my phone was ringing, I had left it in the car that day, as I picked it up to answer it stopped ringing, I noticed that there were at least seventeen missed calls on my phone and a few messages, one of them which read, (is it true about Aubrey) which was one of my boyfriends brothers. Right then I knew what the message was about before I even began to ring my boyfriend's mother, while I was phoning her with all sorts of things going through my head she finally answered, she was quiet for a few seconds, when I ask what had happened she replied that she didn't want to say over the phone, as we spoke back and forth for a few moments, she finally told me that my boyfriend's brother (Aubrey) had passed away. I was in shock, as I turned to look at my boyfriend the look on his face said that he already knew what I was about to tell him. We were hours away from home, my boyfriend had to try and drive home with all this on his mind, the journey home seemed to take forever.

Life was never the same again after that day, things change drastically. The days before my boyfriend's brother's funeral seemed like a blur, the day of the funeral came around. We were all drinking extremally early that day until late that night, after the funeral we decide to go back to our house with a lot of the people that attended the funeral where the drinking continued. There were so many people there, this one man which we didn't know he just came with someone that we did know, he was so intoxicated he just started going crazy on everyone until the whole house was outside fighting, jumping on cars, it was insane to say the least. I was still in the house at the point when everyone was outside fighting because someone was holding be back from going outside. When I finally manage to get away from the person holding on to me, I went outside thinking my boyfriend was fighting, I got about two feet away from where all the madness was happening and realised my boyfriend wasn't even fighting. As I looked up at him I shouted, "what are you doing up there get down there and kick his ass", and as I turned to walk back up the stairs I saw my boyfriend jump over the wall run up the front of the car that was being jumped all over and kicked the man who had started all the arguing and fighting straight in the jaw. The police were called, and my boyfriend got arrested and put in jail for the night, he had broken the man's jaw.

After my boyfriend was arrested most of the people from the wake started to leave but a few stayed, we carried on drinking until late, at this point I was intoxicated to the point where I was ready to pass out, but things took a turn, something happened that to this day I regret, but it was something that happened and I'm writing this about my life and I'm not going to leave out the stuff that I'm not proud off that I have done, cause after all this is my healing journey and doing shadow work is part of that journey, this is a huge shadow that has been following me around for a long time. This one man that stayed, my boyfriends' friends' brother, we were talking in the kitchen, he kissed me and yes, I kissed him back for a few seconds then I pulled away and said that wasn't right and shouldn't of happened, we talked for a few more minutes, then I took myself off to bed, he stayed down stairs with a few other people that had stayed over that night. The next day felt awkward to say the least, as people started to leave to go home the man in who kissed me the night before, left, and as he did, he said "ill add you on Facebook". My boyfriend got released that day to, when he came home, he gave me the look as if everything that had happened the night before was all my fault.

I never told him that his friend's brother had kissed me that night, I didn't know how he would take it, emotions were running high enough as it was, I didn't want to pour more fuel on the fire. I'd say it was about two to three days before I had a friend request on Facebook from his friend's brother, it took me about a day, but I ended up adding him, and we started talking. It was easy for me to talk to him as my boyfriend just spent endless hours on Facebook, not talking to, I barely saw him, he just didn't want to be around me. I know he was grieving his loss of his brother, but we were all grieving his loss, we should of all been there for each other, but people deal with loss in all different ways and that was my boyfriends' way.

Chapter 21 Feeling Alone.

CHAPTER TWENTY-ONE: FEELING ALONE.

I felt alone and talking to this man on Facebook made me feel less alone. After a few weeks of just talking on Facebook we started meeting up, nothing would happen as we were always meet in public, we would just talk and kiss, then go home until the next time we would meet. This went on for a few weeks until the one night my boyfriend's friend came over, we were all drinking together, I must of drank three quarters of a bottle vodka that night when the man I was talking to on Facebook messaged me and said about going to meet him. It was one thirty am, I was so drunk by this time, I picked up a pen a paper and wrote a letter to my boyfriend telling him I was leaving him and that I would be back for the kids in the morning. I grabbed the car keys and drove intoxicated to go meet the man I was talking to. That night was the night we slept together, I stayed at his house that night.

The next morning, I felt like I'd been hit by a train, I sat there for a while thinking about what I had done not knowing what to do next, there were endless missed calls and text messages on my phone, I just felt like I was in the twilight zone. I decided to phone my brother to come pick me up so I could stay with him for the night. My brother came to pick me up, I told him that I had left my boyfriend and spent the night in the car, the next day I phoned women's aid and got put in a women's refuge for the night, this was now the third night I had been away from my children, it was starting to get to me, but after a few drinks to numb the pain I delt with it for another night. This wasn't the first time I'd spent time in a women's refuge, there was a few times before that I ended up having to phone women's aid and be put in a refuge for my safety, my oldest son was fifteen months old the first time I was ever put into a women's refuge, he took his first steps in there. The people who run women's aid are extremely understanding, from experience they were very helpful, they were so nice to me and my son the previous times I had stayed with them is why I phoned them and asked them for their help again. I didn't tell them the exact truth of why I needed help from women's aid but if my boyfriend was to ever find out the real reason why I left that night, let's just say I feared what could happen.

Waking up in the women's refuge the day after, no alcohol in my system, things just hit me for six, I wanted to see my kid's, I'd never been away from them for even one day before, I just wanted to see them. I wasn't sure what to do, I ended up phoning my boyfriend's mother, asking her could I come to hers, she agreed for me to go there. I was at his mother's for about ten minutes before my boyfriend turned up with the kids, I went to grab my daughter from my boyfriend's arms, at first, he wouldn't give her to me but then he did, we sat down and talked for a few hours, we all left together to go back to our family home. After we had left, all I could think about is how much did my boyfriend know about what I had done, I just told him I left that night stayed in the car for the night and then phoned women's aid to help me.

It was only a few hours after we got back home when the police turned up, because I had left the women's refuge without telling them where I had gone, they sent the police to check up on me to make sure I was safe. They were there for a good half an hour then left as I told them I was fine and wanted to stay. The next day things were going through my head at a hundred miles an hour thinking about what I had done and what would happen if my boyfriend found out, for all I knew he already knew what I had done and I was just waiting for him to say something, because if he had of said something I would of just broke down and told him everything. I told my boyfriend I didn't want to be there, I felt uncomfortable being there, all I could think about, is any minute now he was going to say he knew everything, I feared what might happen. We argued for about an hour or so, before phoning my brother to come pick me up, I just left and went to stay with my brother without the kids as he wouldn't let me take them. I was so in my head about what I had done I didn't want to be there I just wanted to be as far away from him as I could.

SHADOW WORK

I'm going to talk a little bit about shadow work and why we need to do it.
Shadow work is a big part of your healing journey, we need to do our shadow work, to be able to grow into the person

we were always meant to be. Take the time to reflect on the things you have done in your life that you are not so proud of.

Write down the things that you did that may have caused other people any kind of pain of embarrassment. Look at what you discover while you are thinking about all the people you may have hurt during your time here.

Face your demons, as they are there to help you just as much as the good things in your life. Everyone has a shadow or two that they will have to face at some time in their lives, when I say shadow, I mean the things that follow you around, the things you brush under the carpet because you don't want to deal with them.

The more you brush them under the carpet, the more you will have to face when it comes time to doing your shadow work. Remember try to deal with any situation as it comes that way your mind will be free of anything that will get in the way of you becoming your true self.

Chapter 22 Drifting.

CHAPTER TWENTY-TWO: DRIFTING.

Five months I was away from the house we once lived in as a family. I stayed with my brother for a while until my then x boyfriend made life so unbearable for him because he was helping me, my brother asked me to leave. I left there and went to stay with his brother's ex-girlfriend. My brother dropped my clothes off there the day he asked me to leave but my ex-boyfriend was there waiting for me to turn up, he told my brother that he would give my stuff to me, but that never happened, he had taken all my stuff threw some bags over people's gardens then took the rest with him and set fire to it. I stayed with his brothers' ex-girlfriend until once again he made life for everyone unbearable, he even dropped my dog off there to me, thinking she would tell me to leave, she was fine with the dog being there as she knew what he was trying to do, he was trying to make me homeless so I would go crawling back to him. In the end he made things so complicated for me to see my children, he would make up stories about the girl I was staying with and said the kids were not safe there, in the and I left to stay with another friend of mine.

That night I left his brothers ex-girlfriend's house to go stay with another friend, he started to try and be nice to me. I could see through all his bullshit and so could my friend, she was good to me the time I spent with her, rent free, fed me, and even let my daughter come and stay when he finally gave her back to me. There were nights the police were called due to my ex coming over and causing trouble, but she stood by me, nothing he did seemed to bother her; she had been through a similar situation in her own life.

All this time I was still drinking, probably even more than I was before I left, "if that's possible", my ex wouldn't let me see the kids unless it was on his terms, I felt lost, I felt like I had no one, yes people would talk to me and comment on how much I was drinking, but no one seemed to really want to help me. When I say help me no one knew what I was going through, dam I didn't even know what I was going through at the time myself, I was messed up big time. I couldn't see any way out, there was no light shining at the end of the tunnel just darkness upon more darkness. I remember one night I was walking back to the lady's house I was staying with; it was early hours in the morning, I looked up and asked for help, I didn't have a clue who I was talking to, but I was talking to someone, but the answers never did come, and I just carried on feeling lost and alone.

All this time when I was away from my home and my kids, I was still seeing the man that I was talking to on Facebook, he was a big drinker to, I know now that was the only reason I stayed. Four months after leaving my family, my ex told me I needed to take our daughter as she needed her mother, he couldn't cope with her, she was three at the time and a mummies girl, without even having to think about it I took my daughter, that same night he came and tried to take her back, but I wouldn't let him. Two weeks after getting my daughter back I slowed down on the drinking until I stopped all together, I was sat there in this tiny little bedroom with my daughter playing on the floor, I just looked at her, all the memories of what I had gone through as a child came flooding back, I'd turned out just like my mother. From that day onwards I decided that my children would never look at me and see in me what I saw in my mother.

Five months passed, by this time I wasn't drinking much at all, not daily any way. My ex and I started talking again round about four and a half months after we had split, by then he already knew that I was with his friend's brother, but I still hadn't confessed about what happen the night of his brother's wake. We had a few arguments while I was staying with my friend, on one occasion he had smashed a coffee cup full of freshly made coffee over my head because of me being with his friend's brother. Even though we were arguing all the time, He wanted to see his daughter and I wanted to see my boys, so we made it work.

Chapter 23 Pressured.

CHAPTER TWENTY-THREE: PRESSURED.

February the 26th came around, my birthday. My brother asked me to go out for the night but I had my daughter now, I didn't know who to ask to babysit for me, my ex came over to my friends house that day of my birthday and offered to have our daughter for the night so I could go out, as we were talking and getting on despite the arguments, I decided to take him up on his offer and went out for the night for my birthday. That night was one birthday I will never forget, I lost my big toenail, had half my hair pulled out from fighting and the worse hang over I have ever experienced the next day from what ever my brother was throwing up my nose and down my throat the night before. I woke up the next day at my brother's house, my ex turned up with two of our children, he said he would take our daughter back with him so I could recover from the night before. I slept for the rest of the day that day.

The next day my ex phoned me to asked if I wanted to come to the house for a Sunday roast, I was a little nervous at first but went anyway. I hadn't seen my oldest son since the day my ex smashed the coffee cup over my head, when I got there my oldest was a little stand offish with me, but twenty pounds in his pocket later from me, we were fine.

My ex cooked a Sunday roast that Sunday and we all sat down for dinner, it was lovely to be with my kids again, I didn't want to leave them. My ex asked me if I wanted to stay the night, because I didn't want to leave the kids, I said yes. That night me and my ex talked for hours, I was still unsure of how much he really knew about what I did that night I first left, I was really nerves about staying there that night. After talking for hours, we kissed and one thing led to another, I still wasn't sure of things between me and my ex but felt pressured into the things that were taking place. The following morning we drove to the friend's house I was staying at to get my stuff to take back home, when I disappeared up the stairs to grab my stuff my now boyfriend again followed me, he wouldn't leave my side as he told me that he thought I was going to talk to the man I was with when we were split, this should have been a red flag for me, deep down I knew exactly what was going to come next, but still I went along with everything as all I wanted to do is be with my children, and going back seemed to be the only way for me to be with them.

The first night I moved back home, all I could think about is how much of what had happened that day I left, that my boyfriend knew, he kept asking subtle questions about that night, I couldn't bear it any longer, if I was to stay there, I had to tell him everything, so I did. That was the start of my nightmare. Every night he would ask questions about how many times I had slept with this other man, if it wasn't what he wanted to hear I was lying, it wouldn't of made any difference what I had told him lie or truth he wasn't going to believe anything I had to say anyway, because what he had in his head already is what actually happened, he wasn't really interested in what I was telling him. Night after night things were just getting worse, I wasn't allowed to go to sleep unless he said it was ok, when I did fall asleep if I woke up in the middle of the night, he would be sitting there staring at me. Like he was trying to read my mind or something. Weeks of arguing about everything and anything, him punching holes in the door just above my head, I knew that this wasn't going to get any better any time soon.

Chapter 24 Guilt.

CHAPTER TWENTY-FOUR: GUILT.

For the first couple of years he wouldn't let me drive the car as he didn't trust me, I wasn't allowed a mobile phone for the first three years after getting back together, no social media, the only reason I was allowed a phone after three years is because one of the teachers phoned him and asked him if they could have my phone number and he got embarrassed that he had to tell them I didn't have a phone. After getting back together he said we should get married, he wanted another baby, again I just went along with everything he asked of me, cause not only did I feel pressured into doing what I was asked I felt an extreme amount of guilt for what I had did and for leaving my kids the way I did.

I fell pregnant seven months after we had gotten back together, even though I had spent every day with him from the time we had got back together he would still ask stupid questions like could it be possible that the baby was this other mans. It was so bad I was even thinking to myself was it possible that even after seven months of not being with this other man, could it be his. That's how he had me thinking. I was seven months pregnant we got married, my boyfriend just wanted to have the wedding as soon as possible so we got married in the register office with ten people present.

 Not the dream wedding I always wanted, I didn't really want to get married while I was seven months pregnant, but it was what he wanted so that's what we did. When it came to arranging everything for the wedding, my boyfriend arrange most if not all of it. When I went to look for a wedding dress, he was with me, I just couldn't find anything I liked, so ended up settling for a pair of trousers and a cream top to cover my pregnant belly, even to this day looking back at the wedding photos you could see I wasn't happy, I did not look like I had just got married, I looked miserable. There was no wedding cake and no honeymoon, I felt like it was just to say that I now belonged to him, and he only got married to me, so he felt more secure after what had happened.

Two months after we got married our fourth baby was born, Simon James, my soul mate to be. Having older children this little man got spoilt rotten by everyone, he was such a happy baby always smiling, loved music, dancing when he got to the age, he was able to be held on his feet, every time music would come on, he would bounce away for hours, our arms would be killing from holding him up so he could bounce away to the music. When he reached the age of about eighteen months, the song gang Nam style came out, that was it, he was hooked, it must have been played at least a few hundred times, it got played that much that by the time he was nineteen months he knew the whole dance off by heart. To this day he is still spoilt, but he is an amazing little boy, unique, I would say that he is more like me than any of my other children, I call him my partner in crime, my little man.

I was thirty-three when I had my fourth child, I didn't drink any more, the last time id had any alcohol was the night I went out for my birthday. This is because my boyfriend now husband had labelled me as an alcoholic so we both stopped drinking. There was no more weekend parties, no one would come and visit us because we didn't drink anymore, we never went anywhere like parties or BBQs, this went on for some years, until we built a summer house in the back garden, my husband now thought it would be ok for him to drink out there, I was totally ok with this as I didn't miss drinking at all, I was to busy being a mother to my four children and now a house wife.

Chapter 25 Faking it.

CHAPTER TWENTY-FIVE: FAKING IT.

When our fourth child was about two, my husband hurt his back moving the shed in the garden, he needed an operation to fix the problem which had gotten worse over the years, from a car accident he had when he was twenty-one. The doctors told him that the operation would fix his back, and he would be able to go back to work afterwards, but not for him, his back never did heal right, he insisted was in pain everyday with it. Because he couldn't go back to work, the money wasn't all that good on benefits, I became his carer to bring that little bit of extra income into the home, after all he needed the care, and we needed the money.

I was my husband carer for roughly nine years, there were days where he would say he couldn't get out of bed because of the pain, so he wouldn't, there were days he would get angry and blame it on the pain he was in, which seemed to be every time he got angry. I seemed to float though those nine years, just living one day to the next not knowing what mood he was going to be in next, if today would be another day that he would bring up what I had done when I left them all those years ago. There were times when we would argue, he would take the bank cards and car keys off me, I was never allowed to leave the house unless I had one of the kids with me, well I could leave the house he never actually said those words, but I knew what was, I knew what was expected of me. This made life hard when the kids just wanted to stay at home and play the x box, of just didn't want to go with me, I would end up having to shout at the kids, so one of them would come with me because of the crazy ideas that my husband had in his head. We had gotten back together got married, had another baby together, but it still wasn't enough to change what he really thought about me and about what I did when I left all those years ago.

Being a carer for my husband wasn't the job I wanted to be doing, I wanted to go out to work, but I knew this wasn't my choice, the way I lived my life was his choice and that's the way he like things, he wanted me where he could see me home with him. I did often wounder if he was in as much pain as he was making out because some days, he would say he was in pain while walking with a limp, other days I would catch him running down the stairs. We were sitting there one day, I think we were watching something on YouTube, they were riding on longboards, he decided he wanted a long board, he had one when he was a kid, so he wanted to get one for our children, so he bought one, but it really wasn't for the kids at all, it was for him.

The day the longboard came we took the kids out for the day, we took them to the park with the longboard, but it wasn't the kids that road the longboard that day it was my husband, he was like a big kid on it, he fell off it that day straight onto his back, got back up and road off on the longboard like nothing had happened, I couldn't comprehend what I had just witnessed, for someone who claimed to be in pain everyday with back pain so server that he is unable to go to work because of it, I wasn't quite sure I was looking at the same person.

Chapter 26 Watching and Learning.

CHAPTER TWENTY-SIX: WATCHING AND LEARNING.

After the incident with the longboard, I started to watch my husband a little closer, I took more notice of the way in which he would behave when it came to his back, the amount of pain he would say he was in. A particular day for me would consist of me, getting up at five thirty in the morning, having my morning coffee, then waking the kids up for school, getting myself ready to do the school run while making sue the kids had everything they needed for the day. I would make beds clean around the house, then do the school run for eight thirty. After getting back from the school run, I would have a second cup of coffee, then finish any housework that didn't get done before I left to do the school run, then I would just sit around waiting for my husband to wake up so I could vacuum. His usual time for waking up was anywhere from around eleven thirty to twelvish.

I wouldn't go out anywhere as the kids were in school, I wouldn't want to be out when my husband woke up, as then I would have to explain where I was, what I was doing, and who I might of saw while I was out. When my husband would finally wake up, I would either just take his coffee and mobile phone up to him or wait for him to knock on something so I would know he was awake. He would stay in bed for as long as he wanted to, then get up have a shower, then either decide what we were doing that day or ask me what I wanted to do, if he had something planed then he would do that while I would occupy myself for the day in the house.

Chapter 27 My Nightmare.

CHAPTER TWENTY-SEVEN: MY NIGHTMARE.

The year 2018 I started having pains and unusual bleeding in my cervix, I went to the doctors for a smear test, I received a letter a few days later, the test had come back that there were abnormal cells and that I had to go for further test. Late December of 2018 I went to the women's clinic to have further test done, they told me I would receive my results with in seven to eight weeks, within three days I got a phone call asking me to attend the clinic to speak with the doctor. I knew, as soon as I received that phone call that it wasn't good news.

It was news years eve of 2018 when I had the appointment at the women's clinic, I went into the doctors room by myself, that's when they told me I had cervical cancer, I could feel my eyes starting to fill up, so I asked the nurse if she could fetch my husband, when he walked into the room he could see by the look on my face it wasn't good news, when the doctor told him what she had just told me he started to cry. After what seemed to be forever in the doctor's office, we left to go home, on the way home he just kept looking at me, we talked about what had just been said, one of the first things that came out of his mouth was, don't use this as an excuse to start drinking again. After we got home, I told my eldest son and my second child, as they were at the age to understand, but I kept it from my daughter as I didn't want her to get upset about it. I decide to have a hysterectomy, I had four children already I was in my late thirty's and wasn't planning on having anymore children.

January 29th, 2019, I went into hospital for my operation, I was only in hospital for two days when I was allowed to go home, that car ride home was horrific, I could feel every bump in the road, it just seemed to last forever. When I finally got home, I went straight to my bed and waited for the kids to come home from school, I hadn't seen them for two days, all I wanted to do is see them. When they got home my daughter came straight into my room and looked at me, she asked, do you have cancer, I just looked at her in shock as I still hadn't told her, when I asked her who told her she replied, "dad had put a post on Instagram and her friends saw it and told her in school", I couldn't believe what she had just told me, I confronted my husband about it as he knew I hadn't told our daughter and wanted to wait until I had the operation, but him being him didn't seem to think it was that much of a big deal, he just laughed it off. He had no right to post anything about what was going on with me, it was something I was going through not him, it should have been me that told our daughter about it not some pay attention to me post on Instagram.

Two days after being home, it started to snow, it wasn't much where we lived so my husband decide he would take the kids up the mountains to see if the snow was any deeper up there. My daughter wanted to stay with me, but for some unknown reason my husband got really angry about it, we argued about it as I didn't think it was fair that he was shouting at her just because she didn't want to go with them, I ended up going down stairs and cleaning because that's what I did when I got angry or upset, I would clean frantically, not a good thing to do five days after having an operation.

Chapter 28 The Good News.

CHAPTER TWENTY-EIGHT: THE GOOD NEWS.

Eight weeks it took me to heal from the operation, after two weeks of being stuck upstairs listening to the kids being shouted at, my husband stressing because he had to do everything around the house himself, I decide enough was enough, got out of bed so I could take over daily life once again. I got the all clear eight weeks later, they had caught it just in time, I would say I was lucky, but I know it was my mother's spirit who was looking out for me as she always did.

Having cervical cancer was just another part of my life that just didn't seem to bother me, I'm not sure if it was because that's just the way I was, or for some unknown reason I knew I was going to be fine. My husband on the other hand drank for two weeks straight, had people over to console him in his hour of need, and took advantage of any kind of attention he could get from me having cervical cancer.

After I got the all clear from the doctor, life started to go back to our normal. There were still arguments, still mood swings from my husband which he always blamed on him being in pain, no matter what mood he was in or what he moaned about that day it was always due to his back hurting. He would wake up every morning in a bad mood, I used to ask him who had made him angry that much while he was sleeping that he woke up in the mood he was always in.

One argument we had not long after I had my surgery, he turned to me and said, "you didn't really have cancer", my response to that was "if I never really had cancer why in gods name was you posting about it on social media", that was the first and only time he couldn't come back with an answer for me. I couldn't take anymore of the mood swings and told him that he had to go to the doctors to see if there was anything they could do to help. The doctor gave him anti-depressants, they did start to help with his mood swings, he stopped waking up in the morning in a bad mood, I could always tell when he hadn't taken them, but the anti-depressants were for his moods, nothing would ever be able to help with his way of thinking, only he could do that, but that was never something he would be willing to do because he didn't think there was anything wrong with the way he was.

Chapter 29 Understanding Life.

CHAPTER TWENTY-NINE: UNDERSTANDING LIFE.

Life was less than exciting; in fact, I was so bored nothing seem to excite me. I would just drift through the day waiting for it to be over ready to start drifting through the next day. If we were to go out for the day as a family, I would have to make sure the kids were all ready for when I woke their farther up, because as soon as he was dressed and ready to leave the house he just wanted to go, he did not like to wait around for anyone, even though that's all I ever seemed to do for him. You would guarantee that every time we would go anywhere there would always be an argument before we even left the house, but still expected to go, after arguing I really didn't feel like going anywhere, I didn't want to go out to pretend everything was fine when I felt like shit, but had to go, or it would just cause another argument.

As time went on something inside me was starting to change, the sound of his voice would really irritate me, I couldn't bear to be around him, and when we got into conversations, I would go off into my own little world, not listening to a word he was saying to me. The conversations we would have would always be about, either something that was on the news, or something he had seen on YouTube, but as I wasn't really listening, I don't recall what he was talking about. My husband wasn't a quiet talker, his voice was deep and loud and always seemed like he was moaning when he was talking. His thought process would just baffle me, everyone was beneath him, the world would be such a better place if he oversaw it, and he just seemed to think he had the answer for everything.

My life was controlled and extremally boring, I wanted to live the life I dreamed about daily. I want to go to work save money to be able to buy a house, have loads of fur babies, drive the car of my choice, which I was allowed to have in my name, and be in a relationship with someone which showed me the LOVE I so longed for. As this was all just a dream of mine because this was never going to be a reality while I was where I was, I just carried on living in my nightmare.

Chapter 30 Getting Creative.

CHAPTER THIRTY: GETTING CREATIVE.

I've always loved craft, so when it came to making stuff for the kids for school, I would be the one to make it, I wouldn't let the kids get a look in. One day I saw this dream catcher I liked the look of, I decided to try to make one myself, it turned out I was quite good at making them, so I made one which turned into many. I also tried my hand at making jewellery, wall hangers and just anything that I could think of, I would make it, I also realised I was a dab hand at painting to.

I started to collect a lot of crat materials, it got to the point I had nowhere to put all my stuff, so I ended up making myself a space in the attic, I loved being up there away from everyone, it was my own space, something I'd never had before. I would spend hours crafting, and just spending time in my space. When my husband wasn't busy doing whatever, it was, he like doing he would expect me to stop what I was doing to just sit and watch tv. I wasn't a big fan of television I only watched a few shows, as I would rather be doing something else other than sitting Infront of the tv.

Crafting became my hobby. I made so many dream catchers, jewellery, and so many other things that I decide to open an Esty account, I tried to sell the items I made. It was my first time doing something like this, I did manage to sell a few of my dream catchers but my Esty shop just didn't seem to take off, of cause my husband couldn't wait to get his two-sense worth in, telling me that I was wasting my time as no one wanted the stuff I was trying to sell. And even though my stuff wasn't selling I just kept on making it as I loved doing what I was doing, and it kept my mind busy.

I know now that even though I loved making things, this wasn't what I was supposed to be doing with my life, therefore my Etsy shop just didn't take off, it wasn't because I wasn't any good at what I was doing, because I was, it was because there was something else, I was supposed to be doing with my life. The universe was trying to tell me that this wasn't it.

Chapter 31 My Awakening.

CHAPTER THIRTY-ONE: MY AWAKENING.

The year of 2021 I was now forty-three years old, all I had to show for my life on this planet was four beautiful, amazing children, a marriage that was just broken down and a head full of dreams. No body knew that this is how I felt, as life just had to go on the way in which my husband liked it to be. Twenty-eight years of my life, I tried to make our relationship work, I wasn't perfect, I had my faults just like everyone else in this world, but I knew that I had given everything I could to this relationship, now I was just feeling trapped, and I was suffocating. If I wanted to do something I would always think of what my husband would think, before I would even attempt to do it, the same with what I wore, he never told me what I could and couldn't wear but that's because I knew what I should or shouldn't wear, he would definitely be the first to say something if I did wear something he didn't like, just like my Herman monster eyebrows, that's what he called them because he didn't like the way I grew them, but I liked them so they stayed. (I rock my Herman monster eyebrows).

The year 2021 was a little strange for me, I started to feel different, I don't remember why but I started talking to my spirit guides. I believe I saw something one day about spirit guides and if you talked to them, they would always answer you, I had always spoke to my mum quite often, but for some reason that year I started talking to her even more, then it turned into spirit guides, and all my ancestors.

That summer we went on our yearly camping trip, we went every year for the past two years, but this time I wasn't feeling like it, but we went anyway. Of cause there were the usual arguments before going, when we got there, and when we were leaving, but when we were there this time I just didn't want to be there, there were to many people there for my liking, I didn't want to be around anyone. I was never a big fan of socialising; I hated being around big crowds and wasn't that fond of one on ones with people either. But this felt different, I, felt different, I just wanted to be by myself, I didn't even want to be around my family, I know that sounds horrible but that's how I was feeling I couldn't explain why I was feeling the way I was as I didn't understand it myself.

Something just wasn't right inside me; I was noticing things I never usually noticed, the light seemed to hurt my eyes, my dreams had become vivid, and the things that were happening around me just seemed like a blur. Life had become confusing to say the least, let's just say I started to believe that there was more to life than what was going on in my life and around me. Magic is not a word I would use daily, but yes, I was starting to believe that magic did exist, the things I was experiencing was nothing other than magic. It felt like magic, it looked like magic, so there was no other explanation other than it was definitely MAGIC, it was out of this world. It was like I was watching a movie, but this was happening to me, I've always known that I was different but wasn't sure why I felt this way. People were starting to bore me, and conversations were irrelevant.

There wasn't anything that I was doing in my life that would cure the burning I felt inside my soul, I just wanted more, more than what my life had to offer. All I could thing about is how I just wanted to go home, I'm not talking about the house I lived in I mean home, where my heart belonged where my soul belonged, this was all I could think about. Life was passing me by, while I waited and waited for that one thing that was missing in my life. My soul was calling to me, day by day the feelings got stronger, the stronger they got the more I wanted that feeling, it was like I was reaching for something that I couldn't quite touch.
There were days when I felt confused, I had so much going through my mind I wasn't sure where my thoughts began or ended.

Those feelings I was feeling and craving more of, just seemed to get stronger by the day, that I felt that one day I would find what was making me feel this way. There were times I believed I was crazy, and even possessed sometimes, until I realised that the feelings, I was experiencing wasn't what I first thought they were but something else. The feelings I was experiencing were the start of my awakening, it was just the universe teaching me what I needed to help me grow. I have now learnt that the universe will never give you what you want, only what you need. I am extremely grateful from the bottom of my heart to the universe; I wouldn't change anything that has happened to me in the past year and a half.

Chapter 32 The Final Straw.

CHAPTER THIRTY-TWO: THE FINAL STRAW.

The year 2021 seemed to go so fast, I spent most of the time in a dream, (that's what it felt like), summer passed then before I knew it was winter, Christmas was just around the corner. That December the whole family came down with the dreaded COVID 19, it had been nearly two years when covid first surfaced in the UK, this was the first time anyone in my family had caught it. It wasn't to bad the kids only felt unwell for a few days, me and my husband felt unwell for about two to three weeks. For me it was just like having the flu but not as bad, but my husband had it bad, I lost two stone while my husband lost three stone due to not wanting to eat anything.

As we were recovering from covid 19 myself and my husband were, well let's just say we wasn't on great speaking terms, he had done something that had really upset me, I just didn't want to talk to him. It was about two weeks I wasn't talking to him for properly, this was really getting to him because life wasn't the way he wanted it to be. He just wanted things to be his normal, but this time I couldn't do it, my heart was telling me to not give in this time and to hold on to what I believed was the right thing to do. That was it my husband snapped, he couldn't take anymore of the silent treatment from me, so he had come up with his own idea of what was going on with me, it was anywhere from me still talking to the man I left him for over eleven years ago to cheating on him with the next-door neighbour. The argument got so heated that he ended up grabbing a bread knife from off the side, he was ready to go see the man next door. Now I know because I know my husband better that he knows himself, I think, that he was never going to do anything with the knife it was just his way of say, "I'm the one in control here, not you".

After that day I knew that there was only one thing I could do, if I was to ever be able to be free from his controlling ways, I had no other choice but to leave. My mind was made up, but how where and when I was going to be able to set myself free wasn't going to be easy, as we spent twenty-four hours seven days a week together, I had to plan it down to the last detail, but even then, I still couldn't see how I was going to take that final step and leave. Days and weeks went by, where I just lived life as normal as I could without anyone expecting what I was feeling or thinking. Everyone thought everything was fine, I treated everyone the same as I always treated them even my husband, I didn't want him to know anything was wrong, not after the argument we had which ended up him grabbing a knife, it was so much more sensible to just go on as nothing was wrong.

Me and my husband has never really had a great sex life, I know that sex is not a big part of a marriage, there is so much to being in a relationship with someone. You need to be totally honest with each other, comfortable in everything you do and say, understand their needs as well as them understanding yours, but most of all you really need to have that connection with them. You should feel when they feel, know what they are thinking without them having to say anything, if you're not feeling, what they are feeling and them you, then it is not the one. It took me twenty-eight years to wake up and realise that my husband was not the one, he wasn't even half of the one I was meant to be with, he didn't even come within a millimetre of the person I felt that I belonged to, I wasn't going to waist one more minute of my life settling for someone that treated me the way he treated me.

Chapter 33 Freedom.

CHAPTER THIRTY-THREE: FREEDOM.

January 2022 was beginning to come to an end, the feeling of wanting to leave was so strong that I knew I had to do something about it. I googled what help there was out there for me, thought about where I was going to go, but just couldn't seem to find what I was looking for. But that's just it, you don't find what you want when you want it, you find what you need when you need it.

I planned to leave on my next pay day so I could have a little money to leave with as well as leaving some money for the rest of the family, we did have much money, but I tried to even what we had out. Plans don't always go the way you want them to, this time was no exception. February the third 2022, my husband was busy that day in the summer house, I knew he would be out there all day. So, I picked up the phone and phoned women's aid, after talking to them for a short time my plan was now in place, I was ready to leave, but this wasn't going to be an easy thing for me to do, I had four suitcases five back packs and about four holdall bags full of all my clothes and a suitcase full of my youngest clothes.

My youngest was ten at the time of me leaving my husband he was in school at the time, I had to get all my stuff out of the house, into a taxi, and down to the school to pick him up and then to the train station to get on a train to the place women's aid told me to go.

Leaving the house that day with all my stuff, with my husband in the summer house in the garden, I thought I was going to have a heart attack, I was shaking from head to toe, I felt like I was on fire as I was burning up from the anxiety. I made it into the taxi, I was off to pick my son up from school, I phoned before I got there and told them he had a dentist appointment that I forgot about, when he stepped into the taxi, he just looked at me because all my bags were in there. I told him that me and dad had a big argument, and I was leaving, to just get in the taxi and I'll explain more on the way. That taxi ride was an emotional one for both of us, I told my son if he didn't want to come with me that was totally fine, I would get the taxi driver to drop him off at the house to is dad, but he decided he want to come with me.

The train ride was three and a half hours long, I didn't have a clue where I had to get off, the only thing I had was a text message from the ladies at the women's refuge telling what stops I had to look out for and how many stops there were before the one I needed. Three and a half hours passed, which felt like a lifetime, we were there, we were at our destination we just had to wait for someone to come pick us up.

I felt safe when we reach our destination, as it was so far away from our home, I knew there was no way possible for him to know where we were, or to be able to get to us. Two ladies arrived to pick us up that day to take us to the house that we would be staying in.

I did it I was finally free from the life that was suffocating me, away from it anyway, being completely free was now something I was going to have to work on. There wasn't a dramatic change that happened over night, but there were small changes that were happening every day for me. When I say change, I mean, I was changing, it was now time for me to heal from all the hurt I had gone through, throughout my whole life not just the past twenty-eight years, if I was to completely heal, I was going to have to start my healing journey from the day I was born.

Waking up the next day after leaving my husband, I knew there was going to be numerous amounts of missed calls, text messages and voice mails on my phone. I never did listen to any of the voice mails and there where loads, I never answered the phone to anyone and only answered some text messages, but only the ones from family members not my husband.

My older children were now at the ages of twenty-five, seventeen and fifteen, one was self-dependant, one was off to university and my daughter was applying for collage for that year. I knew they all had their lives planned out, and could think for themselves, while my youngest was still at an impressionable age, I wanted him to be able to make his own mind up as to where and who he wanted to be with, if I had left him there with his farther, that decision would have been made for him.

We were made to feel very welcome at the house we were staying in by the workers and the other women who were there for similar reasons. It only took about one week to find Simon another school to go to. His first day at his new school, I was so nerves for him, as this was my decision to leave, if he didn't like being in the new school I would of felt like it was my fault for taking him with me, but when I picked him up that day, it was the first time in a long time he came out of school with a huge smile on his face. He loved it there, the school was so laid back, they had chickens on the play yard, and the head teacher was amazing.

We were in the women's refuge for two weeks before my husband had found out where we were, of cause for safety reasons we had to be moved on to another refuge. This was hard for me and Simon, but I just looked at it as it was the universe taking me where I needed to be, I just went along with everything that was happening. Simon was upset because he had to leave the school, he didn't want to go to a different one, I knew it was going to be difficult for him, he was going through a lot as it was, not seeing his siblings or his farther but it was something that I was going to have to deal with, and help him as much as I could.

 I tried to show him how much better life was going to be when we could finally settle down in our place together, that his brothers and sister could come and stay with us, and he could go visit with them on school holidays. We sat down and made out plans of how our own house was going to look, how he was going to decorate his room, he was looking forward to it.

Letter to my younger self.
Dear Julie
It's been a while since I wrote to you last, the reason for this is because you have been going through some life changes.
I just wanted to remind you that no matter how alone you feel right now everything is going to be ok. I promise. Everything you are going through, all that hurt all the fear, lack of LOVE in your life, the not knowing if life will ever feel good, it's all going to work out amazingly. There's going to be some dark times when you just feel like giving up, but it its not your time to leave this planet and there will be so many more dark times you have to encounter. There will be no one there to tell you that everything is going to be ok, there's no LOVE or anyone to hold you when you need it the most, people won't understand the way you are, there will be people who hurt you who don't mean to hurt you and people who enjoy it when you hurt. This will make you question everything, but you will not find the answers you are looking for until you take the time for yourself and go within and search. Only then will you get the answers you have been searching for all your life. This will completely change your whole outlook on life. At first you will question the changes you are going through, but OMG this feeling I'm talking about, it's out of this world, I can't explain it so I'm not even going to try, but if I can let you know now that you're not crazy no matter how crazy you feel at times, (well you are crazy just not about this). I look forward to letting you know how

life is treating you, this is just the start, I can't wait for the journey ahead.
Until next time LOVE you loads your future self.

Chapter 34 The Unexpected.

CHAPTER THIRTY-FOUR: THE UNEXPECTED.

The time that we spent at the next refuge we were in was quite short, but in the time we were there I met some lovely people. From the people who lived there to the women who worked there. There were four women who worked there most of the time, there was a lovely young lady who had picked me and Simon up from the train station the first time we had arrived after leaving my husband, she would come to visit the children and Simon grew quite fond of her. I never told the ladies who worked there but I thought of them as Disney princesses, I'm not going to say who I thought was who, but if one day they were to read my book, I'll just mention the ones I thought they reminded me of, and leave it up to them to figure them out for themselves.

So we had Elsa from frozen, if she ever reads this book then she will definitely know who she is, then there was the fairy god mother from Cinderella, the boss, then we had our very own snow white, you could picture her standing there, singing while birds would land on her, she just had that kind of personality, then there was the princess from Reck it Ralph, I don't remember her name, she had her written all over her, tough, lovely personality, and would look amazing if she were to put on a ball gown, last of all there was naughty little Tinker Bell, she was definitely one of my favourite ladies, we just hit it off straight from the start, she just got me and why I was doing what I was doing, may be if we had met under different circumstances we could have been friends, as she just had that kind of vibe that I was looking for in a person, when it came to meeting new people.

At the end of March 2022, Simon started to have a meltdown, he was refusing to go to school as he hated it there, he just wanted to go back to his old school. This went on for a few days, he was on a video link with his sister, he came and told me that his dad knew where we were, he wasn't sure how he found out, but he said his dad even knew what school he went to, and he would come and pick him up from there. Simon just wanted to go back to his family home, I felt awful I couldn't stand to see him like this, he was missing his dad and siblings, this was something I was doing because I needed to heal, there was no way I was going to tell him that he couldn't go, that day he packed his stuff so his farther could come to collect him from the women's aid office. As he was leaving, he told me that he loved me very much, that he would come to see me when I get my own place, he got in the car and went off to be picked up by his farther.

If I have learnt anything from the past relationship with my husband, is that I wasn't going to be the parent that told their children that they couldn't do something they wanted to do. Never tell your children they can't do something; always tell them they can do anything they want. You might have to tweak somethings along the way, but there's always a way around doing things, telling someone that they can't is not the way. You can do anything you put your mind to and more.

Chapter 35 Alone.

CHAPTER THIRTY-FIVE: ALONE.

It was time to move on again, but this time I was completely alone, when I say alone, we are never alone, but I was the only one that was moving on. Simon was going back to live with his farther and siblings. I was taken to another woman's refuge, it took at least an hour by taxi, when I got there, I was greeted by three lovely ladies who worked there, a few of the women who was staying there, once again I was made to feel very welcome. I stayed at this woman's refuge for the good part of three and a half months, this is where I did a lot of my healing.

The workers at the refuge were fantastic, the women who lived there for similar reasons to why I was there, were lovely, the kids that lived there made life a little easier for me not being with my own children. There was one little boy who I grew quite fond of, he was just under the age of two when they first came into the house, he had trouble expressing what he wanted to say, so he screamed quite a lot, but that was just his way of letting people know what he wanted, I thought the world of him, he always made me smile, by the time I left the house to go stay at another, he was talking a lot more than when he arrived, he just kept on thriving day after day.

There were four women that worked at the refuge, all of which were lovely, there was the boss, she was the one that had the last word when it came to anything that needed doing at the refuge, she had the voice of authority, then there was the other three ladies all lovely in there own right, but there was one that I took a shine to, she was the one I always went to if I needed anything, she was a young lady but knew her job, she might have been young but she knew what she was doing, if you asked her for something, you could guarantee it would be done by the next day, she was the one who helped me find work, helped with my CV, corrected my CV, and found me some where I could call my own. She was also the one who helped me move into that home, she came for a follow up visit to check up on me. If you're reading this then you will know who I'm talking about, you are an amazing young lady, and have a bright and wonderful future ahead of you, thank you for everything you helped me with when I was a resident at the women's refuge.

Moving from house to house, town to town after being isolated for so many years, was extremely hard for me, I didn't like to socialise with people, so I spent most of my days alone in my room, healing from everything that I had been through throughout my whole life. There were days when I would just cry all day, sometimes I would write letters to my younger self telling me that everything was going to be ok. There were days when I would just sleep most of the day away, I was healing, I was giving myself the time the universe was giving me to find myself, and unlearn the person I became over the past forty four years.

It was like being reborn, but with a difference, I had the knowledge of a forty-four-year-old lady to start my life all over again with.

Trying to heal inner child wounds, isn't an easy thing to do, I wasn't sure where to start or if it would ever come to an end. I wasn't an easy child to say the least, I would do things, not so good things to get attention, that was something that I craved the most as a child, because I wasn't getting any from anyone, everyone had their own lives and me, well I was just along for the ride.

Chapter 36 Living Again

CHAPTER THIRTY-SIX: LIVING AGAIN.

May 2022, after endless job searches, with the help from one of the ladies in the refuge, I finally got an interview. The day of the interview had arrived, and I was feeling ok about going, I had come a long way from that day in February 2022, I felt confident. I got to the interview, still I was feeling ok about it, until the manager who was conducting the interview started asking me questions, as they do when you go for an interview, that was it, I went to jelly. The questions she was asking, I just froze I didn't have the answers for her, even though when I left, I could think of a thousand things I could have answered with, but that moment in the interview room, I just didn't have one answer for her, she asked the questions, she answered them for me to. That was it, I thought I hadn't got the job, but a few days later I was invited to go to the induction, to prepare me for my new job.

It felt amazing, it felt like I was getting somewhere, if it wasn't for the manager seeing passed the nerves it could of easily of gone the other way. I would like to say a big thank you to you Annewern, the manager of my first job in eleven years, as a personal shopper, (pick and pack) at Morrisons in Rhyl Denbighshire, thank you for believing in me and giving me the chance to prove I was up to the job, because of that amazing lady giving me that job, I was able to find myself somewhere I could call my own.

My first day at Morrisons was exciting and nerve racking all at the same time, but I was made to feel very welcome, the other employees are extremely nice and great to work with. I have now been an employee at Morrisons for just over three months, I love it there, it has helped me grow with my confidence and I've met a few new people I can call friends.

I love my job, but I feel there is more for me out there in this big wide world. As I am writing this, I have just been excepted to go to work with adults with additional needs. This is something I have thought about for a while now, I am very excited to start working in my new job.

I could have never imagined being where I am right now a few months ago, but I'm here, I am starting to find the real me, the person I was always meant to be. I can do what I like, whenever I like. It took me so long to get where I am today, with endless hours of soul searching, enormous amounts of shadow work, tones of crying to release all those built-up emotions and hours of meditation. People might have said that I was too old to start over, but your never to old to start over again, you can start your life over at any age, its just the sooner you start to do the inner work that is needed to heal yourself, the longer you have to enjoy the rewards that life has to offer.

Who in this world can really sit there and look at their life, and say they are truly happy with everything they have done in the time they have been here. As I know, I'm not one of those who can say that I am truly happy with everything I have done in my life. There were times when I was not so nice of a person, I've looked at other people and judged them for what they have been wearing or the way in which they spoke. I've gossiped and listened to gossip; I've found money on the side of the road but not bothered to hand it in, knowing that it belonged to someone. I've had fights, drank too much alcohol and gotten myself into situation I shouldn't of, I've stolen money from people when I was a child, I've spoken down to people and also lied a few times in my life. But I'm fixing all of that now, I will continue to work on the things I've done wrong in my life and make it right one way or another.

Letter to my future self.

Dear Julie

Only me again your future self. I am just checking up on you to make sure you know I'm still here. I just wanted to let you know your doing amazing, life is good, you are doing what you have always wanted to do. As time goes by, you will find that you will become stronger day by day, and if you're reading the letters that I have been writing to you, then you should be doing better than I ever thought you would. Because at the age you are now, there is no one to let you know that life is going to turn out great for you. So, I am going to be the one that is going to remind you, that you are strong enough to get through all the heart ache and pain that life will throw your way.

Try not to focus to much on the things that have hurt you, as this will not serve you in the future, if anything just focus on what lies ahead of you, and not on what you are leaving behind. Take time to let yourself know that there is a greater good out there for you. Please don't forget that you are strong and amazing, you will become the person you have always thought you were.

Things will not be easy for a long time to come yet, but you are strong, and you will find it within yourself to become the best version of yourself that you can become.

Keep smiling and showing that LOVE you have in your heart and life will give you what you need.
Love you always and forever your future self.

Chapter 37 My View On Life.

CHAPTER THIRTY-SEVEN: MY VIEW ON LIFE.

No one is perfect and who ever thinks they are, are no better than anyone, if anything they are less perfect, because of thinking that way in the first place. We are all made of the same stuff, heart, lungs, brain, kidneys, liver and so on. Our skin colour may vairy, but that's about it we were all born in the same way, and we are all going end up in the same place in the end. If we could only see how much this planet has to offer us, this world would thrive.

There is so much beauty to this planet we call earth, but every day us spirits in our human bodies take what we are given and take it for granted. We were all born for a purpose, one of them is to take care of what we were given to be able to live here on earth. It was decided for us by people thousands of years ago, which just caused a chain reaction of greedy people who believe that this is their world, and we should follow what they think life should look like.

Me personally have never been able to follow any sort of politically correct way of living. If the people who are running this world think they are doing a good job, then they really need to start doing their own inner work to find their true selves, as from where I'm sitting there is nothing, I can see that they are doing the right way. We should all be able to live as one, same house, same income, no one should be treated any different from anyone else. There should be enough food to feed the world, enough medicine to treat everyone on this planet, enough houses so there would be no more homeless people out there, enough clothes to clothe the entire world, but that's right, there is enough of all that stuff I just mentioned, but for some unknown reason, the people who claim to be the rulers of OUR world, decide not to share what we have enough of with the rest of the world.

This is OUR planet, mine, yours, and everyone that lives here. Nobody owns this planet, it belongs to the people that were put here for a purpose, not to the people that have more money than the next person, or the people who think they know more than the average person. God did not put anyone in charge, he gave this planet to us all. Life was not supposed to be like it is, with people fighting over who owns what country, or thinking its ok to let people starve to death, or die from not having the right medication.

Did anyone ever ask our permission, if we wanted all those trees cut down, or the land dug up to make room for more roads because they thought it made life easier for us. I know I was never asked, because my answer would of definitely of been NO. The amount of food we throw away every day would be enough to feed thousands. I just can't seem to get my head around how this world is run; we are all part of this earth, and we should all have a say on how things are done. The people who decides, our and this planets fate, shouldn't have the power they have, who gave them that power, who decided that it was ok for one person to decide on another person's fate, us as a human race should decide on how we should and shouldn't live our lives, not some greedy person who was picked out by another greedy person to make up the rules as they go along.

Life could and should be beautiful for everyone, no one should have to wake up on the streets or wounder where their next meal is coming from, that's just wrong. We need to start again, right from the beginning, and we should decide on how we live here on earth.

I have come to realise, that us as spirits having a human experience, can achieve anything we put our minds to, you just need to believe that it is possible, and it will, be possible. There is something far greater than us, you just need to look inside, you will find what it is you are looking for. LOVE is a word we use a lot in our everyday lives, but who really knows what it really means, who can honestly say that they know what real love feels like. LOVE is that feeling that makes you feel like you're alive, makes you want to get up every morning and just dance, it makes you feel like anything is possible.

Chapter 38 Reflection.

CHAPTER THIRTY-EIGHT: REFECTION.

My time spent here on earth has been nothing but SHIT, but now I'm at this place in my life where I've found everything I've been searching for, my entire life , my life is now starting to become exactly what I have always dreamed about, full of LOVE, excitement, mystery, knowing that anything is possible, I cant wait to move forward and become the best version of myself I can become.

As I sit here writing this book, I have no money, no food, no friends or family around me to ask for help, yet I still wake up every morning full of LOVE, and happiness, ready to face this world with an open heart. I am grateful I have my health, a roof over my head, and the knowing that everything is going to work out the way it's supposed to, because GOD is there looking over all of us, if we just took the time to let him into our lives, we would see that there is everything we need right in front of us.

Life is good, the feeling you experience when you let LOVE into your life will change everything you ever believed in. I never thought life could feel this good, life has been, you could say cruel at times, you could even say that it has broken me down to the point that I thought there was no way back. But I keep going because I know that when you feel the LOVE that I feel, you know you could never imagine life without it, its there to teach you that there is more to life than what we experience in our normal everyday lives. You may not be able to touch what you're feeling but it feels you, and it promises you that you will never feel alone ever again.

Never settle for something or someone that only as their best interest at heart, life gives, and takes away, it's up to you to decide on whether you're willing to except what the universe is trying to offer you. It lets you know exactly where your supposed to be when you're supposed to be there, it also lets you know that LOVE will never leave you if you allow it in. Just feel it and it will continue to help you through your worst moments, it will take you just where you need to be.

Allow the universe to teach you, you will become the person you were always meant to be, I promise. You were never meant to be small, you meant to shine like the diamond you are. GOD has a BIG plan for all of those who just believe in him, he will mend all the problems that have arisen from all the anguish, this planet and the people living here have encountered during their time here on earth.

No one could ever prepare you for what the lord has planned for all the people that believe in him, he will always be there for us all, even the ones that have taken it upon themselves to do wrong. He does not judge, he only has the best of intentions for us all, he will provide what you need when you need it. We all want things, but that's not the way in which the lord works, if you don't need it, you won't receive it.

Chapter 39 Finding my true self.

CHAPTER THIRTY-NINE: FINDING MY TRUE SELF.

There is a light in all of us, all we need to do is go within and find it. Meditate, speak with your spirit guides, you will find the answer's you are looking for. Take a few moments every day to reflect on your life and what you need to change to be able to go forward. Life is exactly where it is supposed to be right now you just need to go within and find the answers you seek. Believe in yourself like the lord does, he will never let you down. He will find you wherever you are, there is no hiding from him, he knows all and sees all. Be good and life will be good to you, just look at what life is trying to tell you, believe in what you want, and it will be yours.

During this time, that we live here we should take notice of what the LORD is trying to show us, we would become a much better race if we just opened our eyes too the beauty that is all around us. Make plans, stick to them, never forget that life is a journey not a destination. find what it is you are looking for and just go for it, believe, that's all you need to do is believe. Find that strength you have always had since you were a child, it's in you, it's in all of us. You just need to believe.

Find the time to reflect on what it is you are searching for, if you can't find what it is then just keep going within and it will come to you. Never let anyone ever tell you that you can't do anything, if they don't follow what it is they are searching for, then they can't really tell you that you can't, because they will never understand what it is like to be LOVED by the lord. Make those plans and stick to them, work hard but always find time to enjoy this amazing planet we have had gifted to us.

People find it hard to come to terms with the fact that GOD is all around us, they don't believe, that's why things never seem to go their way. They are always looking for that one thing that just doesn't exist, it's not the material things that bring you joy in this life, it's the LOVE that is all around us. We look everywhere to find happiness, but happiness is not something you can hold or take with us when we go, happiness is the things that we LOVE to enjoy, the things we LOVE to eat, even the things that we LOVE to do and look at. If I could give you any advice it to never look back and always look ahead of you, you will never find what you are looking for in the past, or even in the future, it's here, it's now make it count.

Place your hand on your heart and hold it there for as long as you can, feel for the beat, listen to it, it will let you know that you are alive, all you have do is live. Take notice of the sound it makes, make sure to be somewhere quiet, and to listen, it will tell you something, something that has been with you ever since you where born. The life you were always meant to live while you are here on earth, if I could find the answers for you I would, but it is you and only you that can find them. The journey is yours and yours alone.

Make it count, make every moment of every minute count, never let this cruel world take anything away from what is in your heart. If LOVE could exist in all of us the way it does in my life, life would never look the same again. Find that thing that makes you excited, makes you want to grow so that you can overcome anything. Take what life throws at you with a pinch of salt, never, and I mean never let anyone take that away from you.

Chapter 40 Teaching The Children of Today for Tomorrow.

CHAPTER FOURTY: TEACHING THE CHILDREN OF TODAY FOR TOMORROW.

Starting off as a child we overlook what is all around us, that's why we forget about what is always been there. If anyone could teach the children of today's society, about the things they need to know about this world, and how to just live off what we are already provided with, then by the time they have reached adulthood, this world would be thriving. Life is always going to throw us in the wrong direction to where we need to go, but if we educate the children of today about what they need to know for tomorrow, their lives and all those that come after them will know how to treat this world the way in which it was meant to be treated.

Today we will find that not only do we take for granted what live has to offer us, but we also take for granted the people that are sent into our lives to teach us what we need to learn. They are sent to us so we can learn from them, we will never be able to go through this life without the help of those around us, that's why we need to go within and find that LOVE because without it we have nothing.

Life is never going to be the way you have always wanted it to be, if anything life will always be what it is meant to be. That's the way in which GOD has intended it, that's why you will never find what you thought you were looking for because it has been within you all along.

Lift yourself up by going on long walks on the beach, or through the woods, or just even down the street, but while you're walking make sure you take everything in, the sounds, your surroundings, everything, let it all in don't leave anything out, its all there to teach you what you need to learn. Take the time to reflect on what it is you are seeing and hearing, make sure to take notes on what it is you find as it will help you gain the knowledge you need to go forward.

Find that inner strength to go forward and make the rest of your life count, look for what it is you are seeking, and it will find you, just open your eyes and look. Never look back ever. Find the courage to make your life everything you have ever wanted, its time to be what it is you were always meant to be. This world needs you and me to take it where it needs to be before the rest of the world destroys it. Teach the children what they need to know now, don't waist another minute letting society tell our future how it's supposed to look.

Chapter 41 If Only I Knew.

CHAPTER FOURTY ONE: IF ONLY I KNEW.

Growing up as a child I knew that there was always something out there, I never knew what it was, but I knew there was something calling to me. Today we need to teach our children that there is something bigger than what we are, bigger than this universe. If only I knew what it was that was out there, I would have been able to of lived a much more fulfilling life. That's why we need our children to know these things, the things I am learning myself and a lot of other people out there are learning today. Believe, that is all we need to teach them is to believe, If I could have known this when I was a child my life would if been different.

I have four children myself, and I hope that one day they will see all the things that I have done in my life was for a reason. I had to leave to find myself, if I didn't leave when I did I would of never of been able to of started my journey to finding the LOVE I needed to become the person I was always meant to be. I didn't leave because they had done anything wrong, I left because I wasn't with the person, I was meant to spend the rest of my life with. He was there to teach me what I wasn't supposed to let into my life, so yes you can say he helped me in a way, but like I said before, if we teach our children what they need to know now, then the children of the future won't have to go through similar situations to learn in the same way.

Find it in your heart to teach them now, so when they get older, they will have the knowledge to know that they don't need anyone, not for anything, all they need is their selves and LOVE. LOVE, yes cheesy I know, but its right all you do need is to LOVE yourself, you don't need that LOVE from anyone else. The earth has everything you need to be able to sustain you in life, you don't need to look anywhere else but within yourself.

If I could go back and change all the things, I had done in life I wouldn't, it happened for a reason and that reason was to bring me to where I am today. Things could have been different, but there not, that's just the way it's supposed to be, GOD sent us what we need to grow, and I have grown so much from my experience. Believe it or not I am exactly where I am supposed to be, here where I am, I was never meant to be anywhere else.

Life brings you what you need, when you need it, and if I could change one thing it would be not to ignore my feelings the way I did. They were there to teach me what I needed to know, experiences are not for nothing, everything is for a reason. Look at yourself in the mirror, and ask yourself what you see, look at the answers you give yourself. Take the time to really thing about what you say to yourself, because it will benefit you for the next stage of your life.

Chapter 42 Self-Reflection.

CHAPTER FOURTY TWO: SELF-REFLECTION.

Life gives you the tools to overcome anything, you can find the answers you are searching for when you meditate, ask your spirit guides to guide you to the place you need to be, and they will answer you, all you need to do is ask. Tell them that you are looking for the reason you are here, and if they could guide you on your journey so that you can become the best version of yourself. Make time to think about the answers you receive when you meditate, they will bring you clarity, so you can make the decisions you need to take the next steps to go forward.

When you meditate, start by breathing in through your nose then out through your mouth, take time to think about what you are going to meditate on, then ask your spirit guides to guide you. After you meditate go for a long walk and think about the answers you received while meditating. That will bring the clarity you need from the meditation. Take the time to breathe in the air when you're out walking it will help, when you finished walking go back and meditate again, this time look at the answers and think about them while you're meditating. This will guide you to where you are heading.

If you don't think you have any answers from when you meditate, then keep trying until you do get the answers you need. Before and after you meditate, make sure your mind is clear of anything from that day as this will just interfere with the answers you get. Time is all we have so make it count, do waist any time thinking about anything that has happened to you in the past, as this has no relevance anymore. All you need is now.

Eat well, stay healthy, exercise, even if its just going for a walk once or twice a week, just make sure you are the best you can be because it will help you with your growth. Take the time to write down any dreams you remember, as this is your spirit guides trying to communicate with you. They will let you know things that will serve you in your journey, and writing them down will benefit you when you need to look back on them to remember what it is they were telling you.

If you ever hear anyone calling your name, never answer them, not even to tell them you don't want to talk to them, this is just spirits that are trying to attach themselves to you. If you answer them, they will attach themselves to you and this is not something you want. Ignore the voices that call your name. If I could have listened to anyone growing up it would have been the one person that I didn't believe in, and that was myself. I never listened when I told myself that what I was doing was wrong, or when I did something that would hurt me. I used to just go ahead and ignore the voice in my head, but I know now that it was my spirit guides, guiding me away from what wasn't serving me.

Never say no to anything that you are offered, it is there to teach you, good and bad. Go to church, take that bus ride to wherever it is you want to go, catch that aeroplane to that destination you so long to go to. Make time for the things you LOVE to do as this will also help you in your growth. If anything, take as much time as you can, to really do the things you LOVE, listen to the music you like, dance like there's no tomorrow, and sing your heart out so the rest of the world can hear you. Buy that guitar you have always wanted to learn how to play, speak to people that you wouldn't normally talk to, listen to what they are telling you, let it sink in as this will also help you on your journey.

From time to time, I wonder if life is even worth living, because of the stuff that people have done to me over the years, but if I could change anything it would be that I was never true to myself. If I was to go back in time and change the worst parts of my life I wouldn't because of where I am now, not only am I happy I am in LOVE with my life that I am living. It hasn't been some of my best moments the past couple of months, but I got here to where I am now, and I am only going to go forward from this moment on. Leaving my husband was one of the best decisions I have ever made, because without him in my life dictating to me every minute of every day, I can listen to what my heart is trying to tell me, and that is to be the best version of myself.

The universe.

The universe is a place where the world is just a small speck, which belongs to a whole other place. There are stars the sun, moon, Jupiter, mars, Uranus, Pluto, mercury, Saturn, Venus and then there is us, Earth. Together we make up just part of the universe, there are so many stars that no person knows how many there actually are. If we could combine all the planets and stars, then we would still only be a small speck in the universe.

We go to other planets to see what they have to offer humans; we travel to the moon to see if could sustain humankind, we as humans are always looking for that something that we feel we need to grow. What we forget about is the planet that we already have, if we took care of what is already provided for us, then we wouldn't have to go and find other planets because we are destroying the one we already have.

Life here on earth is all we need, we don't need to go to Mars or any other planet to see if it can provide for us, we have everything we need already in our hands. Sometimes I think that if we could find life on other planets we would forget about Earth altogether. Why do we do this, why do we feel the need to destroy our planet in the hope that there is a slight chance of finding life somewhere else. We are life, we are all we need, we could do anything we wanted to, if only we would look after what we already have. GOD didn't give us this planet so we can go and find another, he gave us this planet because it has everything we need to live and more.

Every time we send a space shuttle to the moon, or any other planet, we destroy ours that little bit more, and the people that think this is ok to do this, will be the ones to destroy it. We need to get all the people of the world together, and have a discussion, and think about what it is we are doing wrong, and what it is we need to do, to fix the problems we, as humans have done to destroy our world. Then and only then, can we begin to fix what it is that needs fixing.

Take time to think about, what we as spirits, having a human experience are creating for the next generation. The children of tomorrow, will have nothing left to be able to provide for themselves, this planet will be destroyed by the time our children have children, this is not going to change unless we take it in our own hands, and do what we can to save our EARTH, so our great, great, great, grandchildren will have somewhere they can have to call home. If we continue at the rate that we are, there will be no EARTH left for them.

Show them now before its to late, show them that its ok to live a carefree life, that it is ok to grow our own vegetables, and for us to use ozone friendly products. Live is precious, EARTH is precious, people are precious, there is nothing wrong with taking a little time out from our everyday lives, to think about what we are doing, and to try and help fix what humans have done to destroy what we call home.

Chapter 43 Making Your Time Count.

THIRTY-THREE: MAKING YOUR TIME COUNT.

Making time for myself is something I needed to grow, because if I didn't give myself the time I needed, there would have been nothing left of me for anyone else. My children will come to realise that me leaving was for the best , when they see how far I have come since I left that day. They will be proud of what I have accomplished, and what I will continue to accomplish through out the rest of my life. I'm here to make a difference for everyone that I ever meet, and I will make sure that the world becomes a better place for my children, and everyone else's children to have a better future.

There's been times when I've just wanted to give up and leave this world behind, because I have never fitted in anywhere, but I am starting to meet people that care for me, and this makes me feel good about myself. There are a few people that I have encountered over the past few months that have taken my kindness for weakness, but they are irrelevant to my life and my purpose here on earth. My purpose is to make sure that I LOVE as much as I can, because I am made of the light that we all seek, I have so much LOVE to give that I could fix the world with just what I have in my heart, so can you imagine if the rest of the world could LOVE as much as I do, this world would be an amazing place we could all call home.

Over the past six month, not being with my children and the ones I call my own, has been one of the hardest things I have ever had to do, but for me to be the best for them, I must be the best for me first. They are my world, and always will be till the day I leave this world, so the people who have taken it upon themselves to judge me for walking away from them, will never understand the pain I have put myself through to be able to be here for them. If I didn't leave when I did there was no telling what I was going to do, because I already felt dead inside. There were days when not being here was the only way I thought was the way to go, but because I did it my way, I am still here for them, I might not live in the same house but I'm here if they want or need me.

If I could take the pain away that I caused, I would, but it happened and there is no changing the way I did things, like I've said before, there's no looking back, only forward. I can't share enough with you that the only way to live the best version of yourself is to go within and search for what it is you are looking for. Until you do this you will never be happy, you will always be searching for that something that doesn't exist. Look at me I'm now forty-four years old, living in a bedsit, on a street which is less than what you call perfect, no money, no food, having to borrow money to be able to buy stuff till my next payday. But I'm here, I'm the happiest I've ever been in my whole life because I am now free, free to be me. I'm not exactly where I want to be, but every day, I wake up with a smile on my face ready to face the world head on. I'm always nice to people I meet, I never take anything for granted, and I always have a heart full of LOVE ready to share with anyone that is open to receiving.

Chapter 44 Believing in Myself.

CHAPTER FOURTY FOUR: BELEAVING IN MYSELF.

My head is full, full of stuff I want to do, ideas I want to share, and things I need to accomplish. I am going to make it my life's mission to show this world what I am made of, I can give myself everything I need to be able to do this, I don't need anyone but me. There is nothing or no one that can do this for me, I am the only person that can show myself what I am made of. I am strong, independent, and don't need anyone in my life that doesn't serve my higher purpose. People who have entered my life over the past six months, some who I will never see, or speak to ever again, and there are some who I have become extremely fond of.

I have trouble expressing myself when I need to, but its all here in my heart just waiting for me to get to that point in my life where I feel that I can show the rest of the world that I'm here. Writing this book is something I've wanted to do for so long, but there wasn't any way possible to write this book while I was stuck in the relationship that I was in. I wouldn't have been able to tell the whole truth about my life and how it has brought me to the place I am now. GOD has a purpose for us all, and I'm now starting to realise that I am here for that one purpose, and that is to share the LOVE I have inside my heart.

 I would like to say sorry to the ones I have hurt along the way, and to say a thank you to the people that have shown me the LOVE that I have so longed for all my life. If it wasn't for the people that had shown me that LOVE I needed to grow, life wouldn't be the same as it is today. I need to express this because the ones that matter the most have no idea I felt this way, I'm so grateful to them for showing me that I am more than I thought I was. I always knew there was more to my life than the life I was living, and to be able to say thank you to them means I can move forward and grow even more than I have. I will always keep a place in my heart just for them, they will never be forgotten.

Take the time to reflect on what I am telling you, because you mean the world to me, you will never be forgotten never. Make sure you look at yourself everyday and tell yourself that you helped make someone else's life become what it needed to be, just from showing LOVE. My heart is so big, I need to share this with the rest of the world, make a list of all the people you think you might have helped change their lives in some way or another, and thing about how you changed their lives. If you could be anyone, just be the person that I believe you are, see what I see, you will thrive and you will never want to change anything that you have become, because you are amazing inside and out.

Life don't allow you to become what your supposed to be by hiding from it, it will only allow you to be your true self if you show the rest of the world who you truly are. Make time to learn, what it is you need to learn to be able to go forward, you will never be left behind just keep growing, I will be here waiting to see how amazing you have become in the future. Never let that one thing that you are running from ever become a part of your life again, because that would just destroy any work that you have put into yourself. Leave anything and anyone behind if you think that it will not be for your greater purpose.

It's now time to say goodbye, we are all one and you will be in my heart always and forever, please from the bottom of my heart make life count, and don't leave it to long because I am waiting to see where your life is taking you. From my heart to yours LOVE and LIGHT. I LOVE you.

DREAMS.

when we dream, we forget about what it was we dreamt about most of the time, but when you do remember your dreams, write them down no matter what time it is when you wake up, write them down. This will help you on your journey, when we remember our dreams, it is our spirit guides sending us a message so they can help us as we grow.

Make a note of all the details you remember from your dreams, even if it is just part of the dream just make a note of everything you remember.

The time will come when you must look back on what you have wrote about, and it will help you just like it has helped me on my journey. I'm going to share a reoccurring dream

I have had and what it meant to me on my journey.

I have had this dream, it was about this monster that keeps looking for me and just wont leave me alone. When he finds me, he just takes what he wants from me and I always give into him, this happens in most of the reoccurring dreams, but once I interpreted the dream and what it meant to me, the monster wasn't a monster anymore, it was just a normal man who tried to take what he wanted from me. This time I never gave him what it was he was trying to take from me, I walked away from him and that's when the dream ended, no more monsters.
I have been trying to get away from this man in my life for so long, but never was able to say no to him. I always let him have what he wanted, and even after I got up and walked away, he would still try and take from me. This time I didn't give in to any of the CRAP he said or did to try and work his way back into my life, this time is said NO, no to everything.

I'm not going to tell you that it is going to be easy to separate yourself from that thing that is holding you down from becoming your true self, but I am going to tell you that it does get easier. Once you acknowledge what it is that is holding you back, it could be anything, not just another person, it could be a situation that you find yourself in that you find hard to get out of, whatever it is you can get away from it and heal what needs to be healed.

Take the time to look at your life, make a note of all the things you no longer want in your life and how you're going to find a way to banish it forever. Remember, I can't state this enough, just remember to look forward once you start your journey and never look back, as this will not help you get to where you want to go.

If I could go back and change anything it would be to listen to myself, when I told myself the first time that where I was, wasn't where I was meant to be. It took me such a long time to go within and start my healing, that I could have been where I was meant to be years ago. I know everything we go through in life is there to teach us what we need to know, so if we teach our children of today about what tomorrow can bring, then they will not have to go through the same, as many people in this world has had to go through in order to become their true selves.

Find it in your hearts to think about what we are teaching our future, think about what you want their lives to look like when they reach adulthood. Because we need them, we need them to be the humans that we are not. No more hatred, no more hunger, no more killing, we need to heal this planet and the only way to do that is to heal the people that live on it.